PRENTICE-HALL
FOUNDATIONS OF CATHOLIC THEOLOGY SERIES

FOUNDATIONS OF CATHOLIC THEOLOGY SERIES

Gerard S. Sloyan, *Editor*

SACRAMENTS
OF
INITIATION

WILLIAM J. O'SHEA

The Catholic University of America
Washington, D.C.

PRENTICE-HALL, INC.
Englewood Cliffs, N.J.

Nihil obstat:

Harry A. Echle
Censor Librorum

Imprimatur:

✠ Patrick A. O'Boyle, DD
Archbishop of Washington

July 6, 1965

The *nihil obstat* and *imprimatur* are official
declarations that a book or pamphlet is free
of doctrinal or moral error. No implication is
contained therein that those who have granted
the *nihil obstat* and the *imprimatur* agree with
the content, opinions, or statements expressed.

265
0226

161831

PRENTICE-HALL INTERNATIONAL, INC., *London*
PRENTICE-HALL OF AUSTRALIA, PTY., LTD., *Sydney*
PRENTICE-HALL OF CANADA, LTD., *Toronto*
PRENTICE-HALL OF INDIA (PRIVATE) LTD., *New Delhi*
PRENTICE-HALL OF JAPAN, INC., *Tokyo*

EDITOR'S NOTE

This series offers the depth and richness of the divine message of salvation proclaimed to us by Christ. The theology, or "faith seeking understanding," contained here is not on a catechetical level, nor yet on a complex, higher level; it is clear and nontechnical, but at the same time adult and thorough. It is a scholarly presentation of revelation.

These volumes do not adopt an apologetic approach. They neither attempt to justify Catholic faith nor aim at convincing those who do not profess it of the reasonableness of believing. This series is written primarily for those who already believe, who accept the Church as the living continuation of Christ, and the Scriptures as divinely inspired.

The authors do not attempt a philosophy of God or of Christianity, but a study of the mystery of God seen through the eyes of faith. The mystery of faith will not be dispelled by the study of these books. It will remain.

Since some background in philosophy on the part of the reader is needed, and cannot in every case be presumed, there are times when philosophical terms will need to be explained. Philosophical reasoning is very much a part of speculative theology.

Although the breakdown of the series is along traditional lines, each volume is designed to emphasize the oneness of God's plan of salvation and not its different facets. Distinction is made in order to unite. What is taught in the Scriptures is stressed, so that it may be seen how men of the Bible understood the message entrusted to them. The historical aspects of doctrine as held by Christians are then treated: the testimony of the early Christian writers and the liturgy to the belief of the Church; the controversies and heresies that necessitated defense and precise formulation, and finally, the magisterial teaching in each subject area. In this way speculative theology, or the present understanding of each mystery, is not seen in isolation from the sources of faith.

Thus, the revealed Christian message is viewed as the *tradition* (in the fullest and best sense of that theological term) expressed in and through the Church over the centuries—more explicitly formulated, from age to age, and with further applications. But it is still the same saving message begun in the Old Testament and perfected in the mystery and person of Jesus Christ.

One last point is important. Although the study of theology is an exercise of intellect, it can never be exclusively this. The message of Jesus Christ is a living Word, an invitation to participate in the saving event of the redemption, starting in this world by faith and the union of grace, and culminating in heaven by vision and immediate union. This invitation demands response or living faith. The study of the Christian message through theology requires such response, for the message is not something that was heard and assented to once. It is a Word addressed to us that requires our vigorous "Yes" for a lifetime.

CONTENTS

CHAPTER TWO

CONFIRMATION, *page 47*

The role of the Holy Spirit in the history of salvation. Confirmation in the New Testament. History of the rite. Later developments. The modern ritual of confirmation. The effects of confirmation.

CHAPTER THREE

THE HOLY EUCHARIST, *page 69*

The revelation of the doctrine of the eucharist. The eucharist—sacrifice and sacrament. The Mass rite. The eucharist is a sacrifice. The sacrifice offered on the cross. The eucharist, the supper of the Lord. The Mass is the sacrifice of the Church. The eucharist—sacrifice and sacrament of unity. The effects of the eucharist. The real presence. Living by the eucharist.

SACRAMENTS
OF
INITIATION

The Christian sacraments are signs of the power of
God made manifest in the raising up of Jesus in glory
as Lord and Christ (Anderson Photo).

INTRODUCTION

Among the sacraments which continue the life and work of
Christ in the Church, three have long been known as the sacraments of Christian initiation: baptism, confirmation, and the
eucharist. The first and most obvious reason for this designation
is that in early times they were administered together, and so
formed the Christian's introduction into the Church. By them
he was initiated into the Christian community and took up the

practice of the full Christian life. Even today in the West, where these sacraments are not always administered together and where their original order is inverted by having holy communion precede confirmation, one is not considered a full-fledged Catholic until he has received all these sacraments.

But the reason for calling them sacraments of initiation goes still deeper, and "initiation" means more than being admitted into membership in a society. Baptism, confirmation, and the eucharist are called sacraments of initiation because they introduce us into the mystery of Christ. They incorporate us into the body of Christ and make us members of the priestly society which is the Church. They introduce us ever deeper into the mystery of salvation and make us part of the story (or history) of salvation. By them we are taken up into the whole process of redemption, the continuing event that is the "building up of the body of Christ."

The word "initiation" connotes to most of us the idea of something that happens once and is then finished. But Christian initiation is a *process* that goes on all through life. True Christianity is a constant "becoming what we are." Although we receive two of these sacraments only once, their effects are enduring and continuing. They are not mere transitory happenings but dynamic, abiding realities. In a very real sense we are ever being born anew and the Spirit is ever coming upon us.

If this is true of baptism and confirmation how much more of the eucharist, the great, ever-recurring encounter with Christ. For each time that we celebrate this sacrament and participate in it we are drawn more and more into union with him who is the Lord. The bonds of intimacy are constantly strengthened, the love deepened. Each sacramental encounter is a new start, a fuller and more complete introduction into the paschal mystery. In this sacrament the dynamism of our baptism and confirmation is continually at work. It is not too much to say that every eucharistic celebration is a renewal of baptism and confirmation alike.

Centuries of theological development, the fact that first communion is given separately from baptism and confirmation, and the need to defend the very existence of confirmation, have all made us conscious of the distinction among these three sacraments. We find them joined in the Western Church only when young people or adults are baptized by a bishop.

The situation was different in Christian antiquity. The early Christians tended to emphasize the unity of the whole process of initiation rather than the distinction among the individual sacraments. This is beautifully shown by Tertullian in the classic passage from his treatise *On the Resurrection of Christ* (8): "*The flesh is washed* so that the soul may be purified, *the flesh is anointed* so that the soul may be consecrated; the sign of the cross marks the flesh so that the soul may be fortified, *the flesh is overshadowed by the laying on of hands* in order that the soul may be enlightened by the Spirit, *the flesh is nourished by the body and blood of Christ,* so that the soul may be fattened by God."

2

In the early centuries—and even today in most of the Eastern rites—what we now call the three sacraments of initiation were given in succession, to infants just as to everyone else. The reason for this practice was that the early Church saw more clearly than we that the signs are not three isolated events. Although they are three distinct sacraments, they nevertheless form one organic process. They complement and perfect one another. Each has its part to play in this process. One cannot substitute for the other. All enter into the great object of the sacraments in general, which is to make us partakers of Christ and of the Spirit of Christ.

Baptism and confirmation together equip us to celebrate the eucharist. Rightly understood, they are the only preparation necessary for our participation in the eucharistic mystery. Baptism (and to a certain extent confirmation) is the door to the other sacraments. This is true not only because Church law requires that one must be baptized to receive the eucharist but because baptism (with confirmation) disposes us to the fruitful reception of the eucharist. The eucharist is the family meal of the people of God; one must be a full-fledged member of the family to draw from it the full effect that it offers.

To sit down to the family meal one must be at home in the family, sensitive to the current of life that flows through it. Much more is involved in this meal than the physical act of eating and drinking. There must also be union of mind and heart, an attunement to the family's life. The function of baptism and confirmation is to provide the preparation necessary to be one with the family, to live by its ideals and be nourished by its traditions. The purpose of the eucharist is to celebrate, to give thanks for, to commemorate what has happened in baptism and confirmation: the abundant redemption. The Church exists primarily to "give thanks to God the Father who has snatched [us] from the power of darkness and transferred us into the kingdom of his beloved son" (Col 1,12f), "to proclaim the virtues of him who has called [us] out of darkness into his marvelous light." (1 Pt 2,9) The great means of doing this is precisely the eucharistic sacrifice.

The eucharistic assembly is the consecrated means of offering worthy recognition to God for all he has done on our behalf. It is the living memorial of the fact that by the love and power of the Father the universe has been created and summed up in his Word, who for us men and our salvation was made flesh, suffered, died, rose again, and ascended into heaven. It is a daily celebration of the further fact that by the operation of his Holy Spirit a people of his own has been called out to form a commonwealth of belief in the truth and holiness of life. This commonwealth (or community) is one in which we partake of the communion of saints and the forgiveness of sins in the present time, and in which we look for the resurrection of the flesh and life everlasting in the world to come. The eucharist, in short, is the memorial of all God's wonderful deeds, culminating in the passion and glorification of his Son and in the sending of the Spirit.

These wonderful deeds wrought on our behalf become our possession

3

now in the sacraments of baptism and confirmation. In order to give thanks and worship to God for what he has done, we must ourselves have obtained what we are celebrating. Only the free can truly celebrate Independence Day. We see from this analogy that the relation among the sacraments of initiation involves more than mere sequence of time; they have an inner relationship based on what they *are*.

In the pages that follow, when we consider the three sacraments individually we will try not to isolate them from one another. The method of our treatment will be the same with each. We will approach each sacrament from the biblical and liturgical points of view because each of the three is placed in a setting of biblical and liturgical signs which either prepare for its celebration or expand and prolong that celebration. Instead of considering the sacraments as things or as abstract concepts, we shall try to view them as they really are: events in the story of our salvation, actions of Christ and his Church which continue the work of redemption under the veil of signs and symbols. Therefore we will have to study them as they are celebrated in the Church, that is, in their existential setting.

The sacraments must be understood for what they are: the extension of the mystery of Christ into our day and into our lives. They come to us charged with the associations of the Judaeo-Christian past, heavy with the weight of a centuries-old tradition, yet fresh as today.

The essential rites of Christian initiation, the three sacraments properly so called, do not come to us, as it were, unwrapped and unadorned. Each of them is set in a whole complex of subordinate rites which introduce them, comment upon them, amplify, and develop them. In the mind of the Church these rites all taken together are *sacramental* rites because they provide the setting for the sacraments themselves. All form part of the liturgy, the public worship of the Church.

For this reason, and because the sacramental rites are closely involved with what we call the essential rites, they cannot be separated from these except at the cost of weakening the impact of the essential rites themselves. They provide the best commentary on the meaning of the sacraments because they were introduced to furnish the sacraments with a necessary framework. They help us to see these sacraments in their proper perspective, which is the history of salvation. Therefore most of these subordinate rites are biblically oriented. They make use of biblical images and symbols. To read these signs properly means that at every turn we must have recourse to the Scriptures for a fuller comprehension of the whole effect of the sacrament.

Baptism, and in fact all three of the sacraments of Christian initiation, can be understood only against the background of the history of salvation, and indeed as part of that story. For the story of salvation is the working out of the divine plan to repair the damage done by the fall and to restore creation. The ultimate goal of that divine design is "the new man created in justice and in true holiness" (Eph 4,24); God intends "to bring all things to a head in Christ." (Eph 1,10) The way in which that set purpose is worked out is the redemptive incarnation, which was prepared for in the Old Testament, realized in the New, and prolonged through the Church and the sacraments.

The heart of this saving activity is the paschal mystery. The salvation of the world is worked out once and for all in the sacred humanity of our Lord. This is the master key to the whole divine plan. We must be incorporated into that sacred humanity, engrafted into it, in order to be saved. We can live the divine life only by being made one with Christ. Our return to the Father is possible only if we are united with Christ's movement of return to the Father. This "movement of return" we call the paschal mystery; and it is a mystery which we must live. In other words, we have to relive in ourselves Christ's own return to the Father. We must die with Christ and rise with him, that is, enter into his sacrificial surrender and make it our own.

This is the basic principle that underlies the sacraments of Christian initiation. They are various ways of make us one with Christ, of incorporating us into him, of making us live by his Spirit. Through them the sanctifying power of the cross and the resurrection is applied to every Christian.

The one who makes these sacraments effective in us is the Holy Spirit. He is the source of sanctification, the one who enables us to live the life of Christ and who constantly unites us to him.

We were buried with Christ at baptism, in an image
of death so that, like him, we may rise to new life
in the glory of the Father (Courtesy The Walters Art
Gallery, Baltimore).

CHAPTER ONE

BAPTISM

Baptism is the sacrament of new birth. When we have said that, we have said everything, for everything else that one could say is only an unfolding and enlargement of this essential. Birth is entrance into life. Everything begins for the child at the moment the first gasp of air fills his lungs and he begins to breathe. His whole life stretches before him; he begins to exist as a human being, as a child of man.

Baptism is entrance into the Christian life. From the moment the saving waters are poured on our heads we begin to live a new life. We start our existence as sharers in the divine nature and as sons of God. Baptism places us in a new order of things and plunges us into a new atmosphere. By it we enter a new world, the world of spirit.

We became part of a whole new set of relationships and take our place in the life of a community. As natural birth makes us, first, members of the human race and, at the same time, members of a definite human family, baptism makes us members of redeemed humanity and simultaneously members of the household and family of God, which is the Church.

By our human birth we are given the mental and physical powers, though in undeveloped form, to lead a true human life. We become capable of acting like human beings. By baptism we become able to lead the divine life and to act like God himself.

Through this sacrament of new birth, we are born again of water and the Holy Spirit. We enter into the stream of salvation-history and become active in that history. We become sons in the Son, fellow citizens with the saints, members of the body of Christ, partakers of the Spirit, dwellers in the city and kingdom of God.

Baptism introduces us into a new world. It is a step forward from this world into the kingdom of light, "giving thanks to God the Father who has made us worthy to share the lot of the saints in light, who has snatched us from the powers of darkness and transferred us into the kingdom of his beloved Son." (Col 1,12f)

This is the thought that made the same St. Paul cry out: "You were once darkness, now you are light in the Lord. Walk as children of the light." (Eph 5,8) St. Peter expressed the same idea: "You are a chosen nation, a holy people, a royal priesthood, to proclaim his virtues who has called you out of darkness into his marvellous light." (1 Pt 2,9)

For this reason the early Church, following tradition already going back to apostolic times, called baptism "enlightenment" (*illuminatio, phōtismós*). Christ, the Son of Righteousness, shone upon the baptized person and "enlightened" him. "Awake you sleeper . . . and Christ will enlighten you." (Eph 5,14) To be "enlightened" was to be reborn, to be a new creature, for to be born is to see the day.

But no one word or phrase can adequately describe what baptism really is. Its riches are inexhaustible. That is why the Fathers of the Church have used so many different words to describe it, words that stress now one aspect, now another, of this many-sided reality. Individually, each contributes something to our understanding; however, all these words taken together will not exhaust the meaning of a reality which can be grasped only by faith, and even then imperfectly. Only in heaven will we be able to see all that baptism is and does. Meanwhile, here on earth, these other names partially illuminate the meaning of the mystery of baptism, the saving event that continually takes place in the Church.

Saint Gregory Nazianzen gathers these names together in one paragraph:

> We call it gift, grace, baptism, unction, vesture of immortality,
> bath of regeneration, seal, and other excellent names. It is called gift
> because it is given to him who has given nothing himself, grace be-
> cause it is conceded to him who is still a debtor, baptism because sin
> has been buried (etymologically baptism means dip, immerse, and so
> bury) in the water, unction because priestly and royal . . . illumina-
> tion because of its splendor, vesture because it clothes our ignomiy,
> bath because it purifies, seal because it conserves, and is a sign of
> ownership. (*Discourse 40 on the Sacrament of Baptism, 4*)

The etymology of any word is always a help to understanding better
what the word means. But when the word has acquired a whole set of con-
notations, when it describes an activity that has deeply concerned individuals
and peoples, etymology is of little help. We must then examine the *context*
of the word to see what it really means. This is especially true of the religious
vocabulary of a people. The word *baptízō* is the intensive of the Greek
báptō, which means to dip or plunge something (or somebody) vigorously
into water.

The word means much more than immersion or washing in the New
Testament, namely, the introduction of someone into the Church by the rite
of immersion in water accompanied by the words that indicate what such
immersion means. In other words, baptism is a sacred rite that joins a believer simultaneously to Christ and to the Christian community; "baptism,"
consequently, is a new word to describe a new reality.

Even as a religious rite the practice of baptism had its forerunners.
People were accustomed to baptize in Old Testament times. John the Baptist
was not doing anything new when he came baptizing in the Jordan, but he
was giving this ancient rite new direction, for his baptism was a baptism of
penance.

"Baptism" and "baptize" are used not only literally in the New Testament but also metaphorically. The two chief examples are: "Can you drink
of the cup of which I am to drink, or be baptized with the baptism I am to
be baptized with?" (Mk 10,38ff) and "But I have a baptism to be baptized
with, and how I am distressed until it is accomplished." (Lk 12,50) In both
these passages Jesus uses the words in connection with his coming suffering,
in the metaphorical sense of being overwhelmed. Passages such as this
strengthened the idea that Christian baptism was a real identification with
the sufferings of Christ. They stressed that in reality there is only one baptism, and that behind the individual baptism of the Christian stands the one
great baptism of Christ upon the cross. What happened to him there happens
to all of us through the sacrament of the water, which plunges us into his
death and resurrection, conforming us to him in the act of his supreme sacrifice. This becomes even more apparent when we read the rest of Mark 10,38:
"You shall indeed be baptized with the baptism with which I am to be
baptized."

9

BAPTISM—DEED AND WORD

Baptism is the sacred rite consisting of a washing with water and of the recitation of the words, "I baptize you in the name of the Father and of the Son and of the Holy Spirit." By this rite we are cleansed of our sins, whether original or actual, and born again to the life of grace. It is the first of all the sacraments, not in importance but in time and in necessity, for "unless a man is born again of water and the Holy Spirit he cannot enter the kingdom of heaven." (Cf. Jn 2,5; 1,33)

Right at the start we have made a distinction between the rite itself and the reality behind it. All sacred rites are signs of something else which they represent and portray. They are not merely signs such as an arrow or a printed notice. They are always actions, consisting of words and deeds, joined together to form a whole. The words show what the deed means. In this case the deed (the thing done) is the washing with water; the words tell us what this washing is about. Together they make up the sacrament of baptism. Separated from one another they do nothing. Theologians use a pair of technical terms for the word and the deed; they call the washing the *matter* of the sacrament and the words the *form*.

Although these technical terms are appropriate to a theological treatment of the sacrament, many people dislike them because they seem to make the sacrament sound too material and too formalistic. It must be admitted that this objection has some validity. The terms *do* make the sacraments sound like things instead of actions, and therefore modern writers tend to avoid them. Nevertheless "matter" and "form" have a long history and should not be completely ignored.

The first of these two essential elements is the washing with water. Why water? One's immediate answer might be that Jesus wished it that way, but that does not really answer the question. He chose this deed or gesture for a reason. Water is everywhere the element that signifies purification. Water washes away dirt. Therefore it was natural to use washing with water for a sacrament that washes away sin. But that is not all that baptism does. Principally, it regenerates: it gives new life and new birth. By it we are born into eternal life, and no life is possible without water. All life comes from water.

Water can do something else: it can destroy, as the flood waters which rise every spring testify. Baptism, therefore, is the destruction of sin as well as the source of supernatural life. The symbolism of water as a cleansing and life-giving element as well as a power of destruction is highly developed in the Old Testament. It is this threefold symbolism which determined and even demanded its use for the sacrament of the New Law.

Water is used in the Old Testament as a sign of refreshment, of life, and of blessing. To have water in abundance was a sign of God's favor; to be deprived of it was a sign of God's anger and judgment. Especially did the prophets make use of the effect of living (that is, fresh, running) water falling on parched ground to describe the miraculous renewal of the kingdom of God at the end of the ages. The imagery of abundant water is closely associated with the messianic era. Particularly, it signified the gift of the Spirit of God and the fullness of blessing that flows from the Spirit. The sending of the Spirit that was to be the chief mark of the messianic age was compared to the outpouring of water. Water was the symbol of the Spirit. "I will sprinkle clean water upon you and you shall be clean from all your uncleannesses, and from all your idols I will cleanse you. A new heart I will give you and a new spirit I will put within you. . . . And I will put my spirit within you." (Ez 36,25ff) [1]

The devout Jew thought of God as the "fountain of living waters" (Jer 2,13), whereas the righteous man is compared by the same prophet and by the psalmist to "a tree planted by running water." (Ps 1,3)

In the New Testament living water figures prominently in the gospel according to John as the symbol of eternal life (cf. the discourse with the woman at the well, Jn 4) and also as the symbol of the Spirit in the famous passage in which Jesus said, "Whoever believes in me, let him drink. . . . 'Streams of living water shall flow out from within him.'" (Jn 7,38) St. John tells us expressly that Jesus was speaking here of the Spirit who "had not yet been given because Jesus had not yet been glorified." (Jn 7,39) John also relates the discourse with Nicodemus during which Jesus said that a man must be born again of water and spirit (or the Spirit) to enter the kingdom of God. (Jn 3,5) Long, therefore, before our Lord's command to baptize, water was the symbol of refreshment, life, purification, new birth, and the outpouring of the Spirit, all of which are the effects of the Christian rite of baptism. But the immediate reason why Jesus chose washing with water as the rite of initiation into his own community was the baptism of John. The relationship between John's baptism and Christian baptism will be shown later.

The "form" of words used in baptism for many centuries in the West are, "I baptize you in the name of the Father and of the Son and of the Holy Spirit." The Eastern Churches make use of the declarative form: "The Servant of God is baptized in the name of the Father. . . ." These words indicate that this is not merely an ordinary washing but one of special significance, with all the biblical associations of the term itself.

The very word "baptize" suggests what happens internally: a plunging with Christ into death and the tomb, which by his resurrection becomes incorporation into Christ himself. By baptism we are also engrafted into Christ as a branch is joined to a tree. "I baptize you" denotes, "I join you to Christ, I unite you with him, I incorporate you into him." Baptism is at one and the same time incorporation into Christ and into his Church. This incorporation is in fact the principal effect of baptism.

[1] A period between verse numbers indicates that the verses cited are successive but nonconsecutive.

"In the name of the Father and of the Son and of the Holy Spirit" means by the authority of the three persons and in virtue of their power, but it also means that the baptized person is consecrated and dedicated to the blessed Three, that he belongs to them. Furthermore the singular "in the name" is an affirmation of faith in the unity of nature, power, and operation of the Trinity, whereas the distinct enumeration of the three persons distinguishes one from another. All three persons concur in the sanctifying activity of baptism. The priest is the minister, the free instrument of the sacrament, but God himself, one and three, is the prime agent. Like all the actions in salvation-history "this is God's doing and it is wonderful in our eyes." (Ps 117[118],23) Through the power of these words the triune God is present and active at the baptism of the Christian, as he was at the baptism of Christ.

Baptism is a "bath of water by means of the word." (Eph 5,26) The words of the formula are creative words, they effect what they signify. Without them this is a mere washing; with them it becomes the bath of regeneration, the saving mystery of new birth, with all that that idea includes.

BAPTISM
IN THE INFANT CHURCH

From the day of Pentecost onward the rite of baptism has been the means of entering the Church of Christ. When the men of Israel heard the preaching of the apostles they were pierced to the heart and said to Peter and the rest: " 'Brethren, what shall we do?' And Peter said to them, 'Repent and be baptized every one of you in the name of Jesus Christ for the forgiveness of your sins and you shall receive the gift of the Holy Spirit . . .' So those who received his word were baptized and there were added that day about three thousand souls." (Ac 2,38–41)

Throughout the Acts of the Apostles, the chronicle of the first years of the Church's history, the same story is repeated: there is the proclamation of the gospel, its acceptance expressed by the profession of faith, and then baptism. Whether it is a case of individual conversion, such as that of the official of the Queen of Ethiopia, or the conversion of a whole household, such as that of Cornelius, the procedure is always the same. Entrance into the Church is always secured by baptism in water.

In doing this the apostles were of course obeying the command of Christ, for he told them after the resurrection to "go make disciples of all nations, baptizing them in the name of the Father and of the Son and of the Holy Spirit, teaching them to observe all things that I have commanded you." (Mt 28,19f) In the gospel according to Mark, the only other that records the command, our Lord says, "Go out into the whole world, proclaim the good news to all creation. He who believes and is baptized will be saved. He who does not believe will be condemned." (Mk 16,15)

In both these quotations we see the elements of the complete baptismal rite as practiced by the apostles. There is the proclamation of the *kērygma,* or message of salvation, the gospel, which in brief is that "Jesus Christ died for our sins and rose for our justification." Then there is the acceptance of this message, indicated by the profession of faith: "Make disciples of all nations"; "He that believes. . . ." Baptism follows and completes the process of making disciples.

It is well for us to notice that all these elements are present, because we tend to emphasize "pouring the water and saying the words," forgetting the place that the proclamation of the gospel and faith have in the rite itself. Baptism appears, as early as the gospel narrative, as the sacrament of *faith;* it presupposes the proclamation and acceptance of the gospel.

Remembering this will help us to see baptism in the whole context of the history of salvation. If it is the rite that makes people become members of the Church, there must be some intrinsic connection between it and the Church, between it and Christ himself. Christ did not tell his apostles to baptize nor insist on the necessity of this rite for salvation simply because he wanted it that way, but rather because that particular action signified what it actually accomplished. To appreciate what it signified we must do what the early Christians did when they wanted to find out the meaning of baptism: we must look into the Scriptures, both the Old and the New Testaments.

BAPTISM IN ITS SOURCES:
OLD TESTAMENT

The law of the Old Testament in regard to ceremonial washing was based on the doctrine of the pure and the impure. Persons or objects could become defiled by contact with what was impure. These defilements had to be washed away before priest or Levite could participate in the sacrifices.

In the course of time this doctrine was refined. The prophets spoke of the necessity of washing and of being clean not just from ritual faults but from sins: "Wash yourselves, purify yourselves. Put away your wickedness from my sight. Cease to do evil." (Is 1,16f) The prophet Ezechiel goes further than any other in the process of spiritualizing these ceremonial washings. He announces the coming of a new washing which will purify the heart as well as the body: "I will pour forth water upon you and you will be purified, and I will purify you from all your defilements and all your idols . . . and I will put a new spirit within you." (Ez 36,25f)

This is one of the principal Old Testament texts on baptism. The Church has always looked upon these words as the first definite foreshadowing of the sacrament properly so called, as a ritual bath which is administered by another and effects what it signifies. The relevance of this ceremony to Christian baptism is further strengthened by its association with the outpouring of the Spirit. *13*

The bath of the proselytes was another precedent for baptism. This was the ritual bath which joined to Israel the new converts to Judaism, making them members of the holy nation. It was preceded by a catechesis which consisted of instruction in the faith of Israel and by a test of the sincerity of the candidate. A reading from the Torah accompanied the rite, which was administered by another. We can see several points of resemblance between this ceremony and Johannine and Christian baptism.

BAPTISM IN ITS SOURCES: NEW TESTAMENT

That the rite of baptism with water was the means of entry into the Christian community from the day of Pentecost onward is sufficiently clear to admit of no doubt. What is not altogether clear is how the sacrament was administered. Nowhere do we have any exhaustive account of the ritual of baptism in New Testament times. All the witnesses speak of water as the material element used, but they are less precise about the manner of using it. It is not likely, for example, that all three thousand of those baptized on Pentecost were immersed in water. Infusion would have been a more likely method, especially since the prophets, and Ezechiel in particular, speak of "pouring water upon you." Even when immersion was used, it was probably a partial immersion, that is, the candidate stood in the water while the one who baptized poured water on his head. Another reason for this infusion would be to emphasize that one did not baptize himself. It was not merely taking a bath, even a religious one; it was allowing oneself to be baptized, that is, washed by another.

In many ways what is more important than the method of washing is "the word" that accompanied it, since this is what specified the nature of the action and made it a religious rite. Evidence of this "word" is given in the important passage of St. Paul's epistle to the Ephesians: "Christ loved the Church and delivered himself up for her in order to sanctify her, purifying her by the bath of water with the word." (Eph 5,25f)

What was this "word" that accompanied the washing with water? We must avoid reading back into New Testament times the liturgical practices and the theological doctrines of our own time. "Word" here almost certainly means more than what we call the "form," or the words, of baptism. In the New Testament, "word," especially when it is used in connection with baptism, means the *kērygma*, the proclamation of the good news of salvation which the hearer must accept before he can be admitted to baptism. This proclamation and this profession of faith formed an important part of the formula by which baptism was administered. The necessary link between the word proclaimed and the rite of baptism is brought out in the words of our Lord in the command to baptize: "Proclaim the gospel to every creature. He *who believes* and *is baptized* will be saved." (Mk 16,16) We see the order of procedure clearly indicated here. First the *kērygma,* then acceptance of the *kērygma,* and finally baptism. The same order is shown in the words of the first chapter of St. Paul to the Ephesians: "After you heard the word of truth, the good news of your salvation, you believed in it and you were marked with the seal of the Spirit of promise." (Eph 1,13f)

The rite of baptism, therefore, came at the end of the preaching of the gospel and after a personal adherence to that gospel made in the profession of faith. It is very important for us to understand this because it brings out the link that existed (and should always exist) between faith and baptism. Baptism is not a magic rite but a *personal encounter with Christ,* preceded by a *personal encounter in the word* proclaimed and heeded. Just as John the Baptist associated his baptism with his prophetic message, the Church associated her own baptism with the proclamation of the good news and with the adherence of faith to this word of truth.

The word of the message of salvation comes first. The primitive prebaptismal catechesis was built around it. It was expressed in brief formulas which were easy to learn, such as, "Jesus is Lord" (that is, risen from the dead and therefore fully divine in power), or "Christ himself died once for our sins, the just for the unjust, in order to lead us to God. Put to death in the flesh, he was brought to life in the spirit." (1 Pt 3,18) This is the meaning of "the proclamation of the name" which St. Paul speaks of in Romans 1,4f. "To proclaim the name" is to proclaim the gospel of the resurrection of Christ.

The second step of the process was to accept the proclamation of the *kērygma* by faith. We read in the Acts of the Apostles about those who heard the preaching of St. Peter at Pentecost: "They therefore receiving the word submitted to baptism" (Ac 2,41); and more explicitly later on in the eighth chapter: "Philip said, 'If you believe with your whole heart it can be done' (that is, is lawful). But he answered, 'I believe that Jesus Christ is the Son of God.'" (Ac 8,37) This and other passages allow us to conclude that some kind of profession of faith in the name of Jesus preceded baptism. Faith here includes the idea of conversion, of a total adhering to Christ.

Last of all, after the word of the *kērygma* and the word of the profession of faith, came the word of the baptismal formula itself. Here we encounter the difficulty that we do not know for certain what the words of the baptismal formula were. Exegetes and historians of the ritual are divided on this point. Some think that the expression "baptized in the name of Jesus" (Ac 10,42–48 and similar passages) designated a real formula of baptism; others think that the trinitarian formula in Matthew 28,19 was always used.

Whatever the formula used, it would express the idea of a personal adherence to the name of Jesus by a profession of faith in one way or another. The oldest formulas that we know about definitely date from the third century. These are not in the declarative form that we know today; they are in the form of questions. Nevertheless they are in accord with the command of our Lord to baptize in the name of the Father, and of the Son, and of the

Holy Spirit. That command should not be understood to stipulate the exact words to be used, but rather to describe the nature of baptism and to show what it does.

"Baptism in the name of Jesus" therefore designates baptism insofar as it is adherence to Christ, or as distinguished from the baptism of John.

The Baptism of John

The work of John the Baptist is significant because he is the forerunner, the one specifically chosen to usher in Christ's messianic mission.

"And he will go before him in the spirit and power of Elia to turn the hearts of the fathers to the children and the disobedient to the wisdom of the just, to make ready for the Lord a people prepared." (Lk 1,17) John prepared the way for Jesus not only by his preaching but by the highly significant rite of baptism. In fact the chief title given him in the gospels, as if to sum up all his achievement in that one word, is "the baptizer" or "the baptist."

The whole content of his preaching is summarized in Mark's gospel as "the baptism of repentance." (Mk 1,4) "And crowds were baptized by him in the Jordan, confessing their sins." (Mk 1,5) This is a symbolic action, of the kind so loved by the Jews and so suited to the Hebrew mentality. The action meant that to be a real Israelite, to flee from the wrath to come and to get right with God, it was necessary to undergo cleansing, both ritual and moral.

The moral cleansing was symbolized by the ritual act and was not to be separated from it. John's baptism was therefore a real washing in the Jordan, symbolic of repentance and accompanied by conversion, *metánoia*, change of mind and heart. John was the last of the prophets, and his message was, in the ancient prophetic tradition: "Return, O Israel, return to the Lord, your God." (Os 14,2) His action was consistent with the prophetic symbolical acts: "Repent, for the kingdom of heaven is near at hand." (Mt 3,2) He made use of the baptism of the proselytes and gave it a new meaning.

At the same time what John did was not an end in itself; it was only the preparation for the still greater baptizer and baptism that are in prospect. "I baptize in water, but there is one who is to come after me who is more powerful than I . . . He will baptize in the Holy Spirit and in fire." (Mt 3,11)

John came to bring about "a people prepared." His baptism got ready for a work but did not accomplish that work. Nevertheless it was a foreshadowing of what that other baptism would be. The cleansing of John's baptism was a token of that radical internal cleansing and renewal that would be accomplished by a similar action, and that would be a complete purification which would inaugurate a new world.

The baptism of John may be compared to the baptism of the proselytes which introduced converts to Judaism into the people of Israel. It incorporated those who received it into the true posterity of Abraham, those who, like

Abraham, believed in the one God. It joined them to the remnant of Israel which was henceforth withdrawn from the wrath of God and awaited the coming Messia.

John's baptism was a once-for-all action given by another and received with a view to repentance and pardon. It involved the confession of sins and an effort at the definitive conversion the rite was intended to express. It meant for those who underwent it that the present world had become bankrupt, that it was condemned and under sentence. Thus, it signified the end of the age, and the beginning of a new way of life.

There is a continuity and a resemblance between John's baptism and Christian baptism. Both were in the same line of development. Both involved being baptized in water by another, and were conferred after the proclamation of the divine message announcing the messianic times. Both were a "baptism of repentance" which marked the beginning of a new life for those who received them. Both made men enter a community of disciples and inaugurated a new way of living.

Nevertheless, the differences far exceed the resemblances. A closer examination shows that the baptism of John consistently falls short of Christian baptism. It is the shadow, whereas "baptism in Jesus' name" is the reality. The "friend of the bridegroom" must not be confused with the Bridegroom himself. John's baptism was a call to repentance but it could not effect repentance. It signified a change of heart but did not bring that change about. Only Christ's baptism could do that, because Christ's baptism is in the Holy Spirit. The gift of the Spirit makes the difference. Christian baptism is a baptism into the glorified humanity of Christ. John himself put his finger on this difference when he said "I baptize with water, but He will baptize you with the Holy Spirit." (Mk 1,8) The washing with water in Jesus' name is the outward sign of the true inward washing that is done by the power of the Spirit. Christian baptism does more than introduce one into a new way of life: it effects a radical transformation and is a new birth because it joins us to the death and resurrection of Christ.

Between the baptism given by John and Christian baptism stands the event that makes the difference between them: the death and resurrection of Christ and the consequent sending of the Spirit. Only when Jesus had been glorified could baptism have its effect.

The Baptism of Jesus

Our Lord's baptism in the Jordan is an event of the greatest significance. It was one of the biggest events of his life and is of prime importance for an understanding of that life. It literally tells us everything about him and his mission. We can see its significance from the prominence given to it by each of the evangelists.

The baptism of Jesus was at once the announcement of his death upon the cross and the preparation for it. At the same time it pointed to the future relationship between Christian baptism and the death and resurrection of Jesus. Basic to the whole event is the idea that both Messia and messianic community must undergo the same experience: the death and the resurrection. Therefore the baptism of Jesus marks the inauguration of his messianic mission which was "to seek and to save that which is lost." (Lk 19,10)

"To make ready for the Lord a people prepared" was John's mission. The way he fulfilled it was to gather the messianic people together by a baptism of repentance (*metánoia*), thus getting them ready for the messianic outpouring of the Spirit. Jesus submitted himself to the baptism of John although he had no need of repentance, but, as he said himself, "to fulfill all righteousness." (Mt 3,15) That is, he submitted himself to the will of his heavenly Father. To carry out the plan of salvation he had to station himself among sinners, for he was the Lamb of God who would take away the sins of the world by taking those sins upon himself. By his baptism he identifies himself with the community he came to save.

Furthermore, as the phrase indicates, Jesus had to submit to *another* kind of baptism "in order to fulfill all righteousness." That baptism was his death on the cross. The act of being submerged in the water of the Jordan suggested to him the pain and anguish that would overwhelm him on the cross, and the burial in the water prefigured his burial in the tomb. But at the same time, as he came out of the water the Spirit rested upon him in the form of a dove. This part of the incident suggests his emergence from the tomb and his glorification at the right hand of the Father.

The teaching underlying the whole event is clear: it is at once a dramatization in advance of the redemptive event, and a demonstration of how that redemptive event is to be applied to the community. The early Church grasped very soon the link between the baptism of Jesus in the Jordan, the baptism in blood upon the cross, and the baptism in water "in the name of Jesus." We have here, in fact, the classic Christian pattern of redemptive events: the foreshadowing, the realization, the sacrament.

What we have seen shows us that the instinct of the early Church to depict the baptism of Christ in the baptisteries was a correct one. Church law still requires that such a representation be in every baptistery, on or near the font. There is a definite link between the baptism of Jesus and our baptism. The link is the cross. Behind every Christian baptism stands the one baptism on the cross, a fact we give expression to when we say, "I confess one baptism for the remission of sins."

THE RITE OF BAPTISM

Because the sacraments are signs that effect or produce what they signify, we must study the meaning and content of the sign in order to learn what these effects are. This means the study of the *full* sign, of the *whole* rite, the words no less than the deeds that compose it. Furthermore, this study is not confined to what the theologians call the essential matter and form of the sacrament. Rather it embraces the whole setting in which the sacrament comes to us.

The study of baptism necessarily involves the study of Lent and its themes, the Easter vigil, the blessing of the baptismal water, the Masses of Easter and the Easter Octave, as well as the introductory and concluding parts of the baptismal rite itself, because in a broad sense these are all part of the sign. They comment upon and expand the meaning of the central rite. They illuminate the meaning of "I baptize you" and provide the setting and background of the sacrament itself.[2]

The sacraments are not isolated events but are all part of a vast "mysterium" or "sacramentum" which embodies and contains the mystery of Christ in its fullness. The sacraments themselves are, as it were, heightened moments of this one great mysterium. But all the rites which enshrine the central sacramental realities partake—each in its own way—of the dignity and sacramentality of those seven streams we know as sacraments properly so called. For purposes of theological accuracy it is necessary for us to distinguish between what is essential and what is nonessential. But theological accuracy is not the only thing we must consider. Equally important is our right appreciation of the riches of sacramental life. This can be had only by seeing the sacrament in its biblical and liturgical setting.

The biblical and liturgical setting of baptism is next in importance to that of the eucharist. Once the ritual of the sacrament had developed—by the fifth century at the latest—baptism formed part of a vast complex of sacred rites which led up to it, commented upon its actual celebration, and prolonged that celebration.

The catechumenate itself was bound up with the celebration of Lent. This was true to such an extent that even today Lent is incomprehensible apart from baptism, while the modern ritual of baptism bears more than one trace of the influence of the discipline of the catechumenate. Because this period of time coincided with the preparation for baptism, the Lenten liturgy as we know it is still infused with the great baptismal themes. Baptism (and confirmation and the eucharist) was administered as a rule only during the great Easter vigil. Consequently the Easter vigil, especially at Rome, became a great baptismal celebration; the consecration of the water and all the main rites of baptism took place during that night. This custom has left its mark upon our Easter vigil even today and explains why it is impossible to understand the meaning of the Easter vigil without having a rather complete grasp of the theology of baptism.

In dealing with the ritual of baptism we must constantly remember that what is now done in the space of a few minutes was once spread out over

[2] In the same way the Roman missal, with its readings, chants, and prayers, is the best commentary we have on the eucharistic rite. The liturgical books of the other rites are likewise invaluable for a better understanding of the eucharist of the Roman rite.

several years. Many of these rites lose much of their meaning under present circumstances, which is why liturgical scholars have long wished that their original spacing could be restored. The Holy See granted this wish for adult baptism in 1962, but the permission of the ordinary is required.

The modern rite of baptism is contained in the *Rituale Romanum,* first issued by Pope Paul V in 1614. Actually there are two rituals for baptism, a longer one for the baptism of adults and a shorter one for infants. But in reality both these rituals consist of formularies written originally for adults; it is a curious anomaly that there is no real ritual for the baptism of children. Almost all the formulas presuppose that the candidate is fully grown and that he is capable of understanding what is happening. The *Constitution on the Sacred Liturgy* (December 4, 1963) is the first official recognition of the need for a revision of the rite of the baptism of infants. "The rite for the baptism of infants is to be revised, and it should be adapted to the circumstance that those to be baptized are, in fact, infants." (Art. 67) Actually, both rituals badly need revision, for the modern rite of baptism is far from satisfactory and needs to be simplified. As it stands, its formulas for the most part make sense only when we examine the history of the rite.

The Catechumenate

Some preparation has always been presupposed for adult baptism but there was no formal organization of that preparation before the third century. The first converts to Christianity were nearly all Jews or those devout pagans called "godfearers" in the Acts of the Apostles. They had been preparing for this great moment in their lives for years, because the synagogue services had given them a thorough instruction in the history of salvation. They knew all about the Messia, the kingdom, the promises. They knew, too, what kind of response was expected to the demand for repentance and conversion that accompanied the preaching of baptism in the early Church.

Those who would not have been ready for Christianity's message through familiarity with the Scriptures and Jewish thought patterns would have been in need of extended instruction in all these matters. It was given by a chief catechist who had the title "instructor of the hearers." In reality, this instruction was the special responsibility of the bishop, but he often delegated it.

The length of the catechumenate varied, but it was never short. It was made up of a series of instructions consisting mainly of "hearing the word" from a teacher. Each session ended with prayer, the catechumens praying apart from the believers. The teacher then gave them his blessing by laying his hand upon them. Catechumens were allowed to take part in the synaxis, or "service of the word," but not in the eucharistic action. By the end of the second century, therefore, if not earlier, a lengthy period of preparation was organized in the Church. This new institution was called the catechumenate and those undergoing it were known as catechumens, from the Greek word *katēchein,* meaning "to instruct." We should note that the catechumen was not only instructed in the Christian faith, but was also gradually initiated into Christian life and ways. The Church taught him how to pray and opened up the Scriptures to him.

The emphasis was upon moral formation rather than doctrinal instruction. In fact the whole program was a process of spiritual formation comparable to that given in a strict religious novitiate today. Tertullian calls the catechumenate the novitiate of the Christian life. (*On Penance,* 6) The other source of our knowledge about the catechumenate of the primitive Church besides Tertullian is the *Apostolic Tradition* of St. Hippolytus of Rome (ca. 215), which represents a more developed phase of the institution.

A candidate had to prove himself even before he was admitted to the catechumenate. He presented himself to the leaders of the Church accompanied by a member of the Church who guaranteed his good intentions. He had to show that he was not engaged in any trade or profession that would be incompatible with the Christian life. If he was admitted to the catechumenate he was considered a Christian, but not a *"fidelis."* He underwent instruction from the *"doctores ecclesiae"* and assisted at the first part of the Mass.

The catechumenate normally lasted three years. Before one could be admitted to baptism, he was examined chiefly on the conduct of his life during that time. If he passed this examination he was exorcised every day for a brief period, then finally baptized during the Easter vigil.

In the course of the Lenten observance (at various times, three, six, and eight weeks in length) two solemn rites took place: the *traditio symboli* and the *traditio orationis dominicae.* The first of these was the "handing over" of the apostles' creed (*symbolum*) and consisted in the teaching of the various articles of the creed to the "chosen" in the framework of a solemn liturgical gathering. The elect had to learn this creed by heart as one would a password. In fact this is what *symbolum* means: password.

In Africa the rite took place after the Scripture readings of the Mass of the fourth Sunday of Lent; this Mass was later transferred to the following Wednesday. Even to this day the texts of this Mass are filled with references to baptism. The day was called *"in aurium aperitione,"* "Sunday of the Opening of the Ears," because this was the day that the catechumens were to hear the truths of faith for the first time.

The second solemn rite which took place during the Lenten season was the *traditio-redditio* ("handing over" and "giving back") of the Our Father. This too consisted of an explanation of that prayer phrase by phrase. The candidate learned it by heart and recited it before the congregation after he had recited the creed. This rite originated in Africa but was later adopted at Rome. Again we see a survival of it in the modern baptismal ritual where the candidate is directed to say the Lord's prayer after the creed. Normally we would say the Our Father first, but we preserve the original arrangement in this one place.

Besides the *traditio* of the creed and the Our Father, Rome added the *traditio evangelii,* the "handing over of the gospel." This consisted of the reading of the gospels accompanied by homilies by the bishop. The idea was to impart to the catechumens the substance of the gospel teaching as the Torah of the new covenant, the abiding guide of the Christian life. This rite has disappeared altogether from the modern baptismal ritual but there is a reference to it in the phrase, "moved by the pleasing fragrance of your teachings."

The threefold renouncing of Satan is an impressive rite today but in times past it was even more so. The candidate first turned his face to the West, the abode of darkness, the place where the sun sets. Then he was asked by name if he renounced Satan. The question was put directly to him and he could not evade it. To follow Christ means to renounce the devil. No man can serve two masters. The Christian profession means a complete break with sin and an entire conversion to God.

The candidate renounced Satan three times. This rite summarized the "scrutinies" or exorcisms which had been spread over the Lenten season, and was intended to correspond in reverse to the threefold interrogation on the faith which preceded (or accompanied) the actual baptism. The candidate renounced first Satan, then all his works, and finally all his "pomps." This last word originally referred to the procession or parade at the games in the circus, which was a symbol of the pagan spectacles and the idolatrous ceremonies that the devil used to lure men into his service. It is translated now as "display" or "allurements."

By this threefold renunciation the catechumen emancipated himself from the devil's power and bound himself personally to put off "the old man," that is, his lower nature and all evil conduct, and to set aside the works of darkness and live no longer according to the prince of this world.

The anointing of the catechumens with oil, which followed immediately, is related to the same general idea. The oil is the oil of combat intended to prepare the athlete of Christ for his lifelong struggle against the powers of evil.

Today the priest anoints the catechumen on the breast and between the shoulder blades. But in ancient times the candidate was stripped and anointed over the whole body (by deaconesses in the case of women). This fact also indicates the purpose of this anointing, for it was the practice in antiquity for athletes (wrestlers) to be smeared with oil over the whole body to prepare them for the contest. As St. Ambrose says in his catechetical sermons *On the Sacraments:* "You have been anointed as an athlete of Christ, as if you were about to engage in some profane struggle. You have professed your willingness to undertake a contest." (2,2f)

Although this anointing is greatly reduced today the rite still has the same significance. The one who is baptized enters into a continuing battle against Satan.

By the thirteenth century all special meetings (the scrutinies) in preparation for baptism had been eliminated, largely because of the custom of baptizing infants soon after birth. The rites themselves were not eliminated, but were compressed into one ceremony held immediately before the baptism. This practice lasted into our own day when it was modified, first by allowing the introductory ceremonies to be performed in the morning when someone was to be baptized at the Easter vigil, then by the restoration in 1962 of the earlier system of having these rites spread out over a period for adult converts.

The Paschal Vigil

From ancient times through the ninth century (even later in some places), baptism was normally celebrated during the vigil on Easter eve. The reason for this is obvious. Easter is the great feast of our redemption, celebrating both the death and the resurrection of Christ. Baptism is the way in which we lay hold of the redemption, the means by which the saving power of the death and resurrection is applied to us. It was therefore eminently fitting that baptism should be given on this night, which still remains the ideal time for baptism, at least for adults. Both the *Code of Canon Law* (1918) and the restored Order of Holy Week (November, 1955) recommend this practice.

The whole structure of the paschal vigil presumes that baptism (and confirmation), as well as the eucharist, is being celebrated that night. Even for those who have already been baptized the Easter vigil is the great means of recalling and celebrating their own baptism and renewing the spirit of that baptism. This is one reason why the new Order of Holy Week provides for the renewal of baptismal promises on this night.

Seen in this perspective the paschal candle takes on increased meaning. Not only is it the symbol of the risen Christ but it represents also the "illumination," the enlightenment, that takes place in baptism. The "true light that enlightens every man" does this enlightening primarily in baptism. By baptism we become "children of the light" and so "children of the resurrection"; that is, the light and resurrection of Christ are the source of light and life for us.

The relationship between the pasch of the Old Testament and the Christian paschal feast is brought out in the *Exsultet*, the paschal hymn. The passage of Christ from death to glorious life was prefigured by the passage of the Israelites through the Red Sea. Now Christ's passage is re-enacted in his Church through and by the sacraments celebrated on this night. The sacred mysteries of baptism and the eucharist "separate believers in Christ from the vices of the world and the darkness of sin, restore them to grace, and join them to holiness." Baptism (the "sanctification of this night") puts all evil to flight, washes away sins, restores innocence to the fallen and joy to those who mourn. "On this night heaven is joined to earth and the divine to the human."

23

THE READING   Traditionally the Easter vigil constituted the immediate preparation for the Christian initiation by prayer and meditation on the Scriptures, especially the Old Testament prefigurations of the Christian mysteries. These readings varied from place to place and from time to time, but certain main events and incidents recurred regularly. Some of these have survived in the restored Holy Week Order, others have disappeared.

The favorite readings were as follows. First, the account of creation was read to show that baptism is the new creation. The next reading was the account of the deluge, which symbolized the destruction of vice and the beginning of a new world of grace. Noah and his ark were favorite types of the saving effects of salvation in the early Church. Naturally, the Exodus account would find a place in such a series, because of all Old Testament types the Exodus was the preferred prefiguration of the redemption, the resurrection, and baptism. As early as the time of St. Paul, the crossing of the Red Sea was considered one of the types of baptism. The Canticle of Moses sung after this lesson was rightly regarded by the early Church as a prophecy of the victory of Christ and the Christian. We notice that in the Apocalypse John has the redeemed, who have passed over to the other side, singing the Canticle of Moses as their song of triumph.

In succession, congregations heard the account of the sacrifice required of Abraham, the renewal of the covenant from Deuteronomy, the reading from Isaia about the remnant and the vineyard of Yahweh, and the account of the vision of the dry bones from Ezechiel 37. This last selection is a prophecy of the lifegiving activity of the Holy Spirit who works through the three sacraments of Christian initiation. It is also a prophecy of the resurrection of Israel, which amounts to the same thing because the Holy Spirit is the Spirit of the resurrection.

THE CONSECRATION OF THE BAPTISMAL WATER   The blessing of the water to be used for baptism is a superb example of the power of the liturgy to teach and inspire. It is part of the full sign of baptism. To study it is to gain a rich insight into what baptism does. It is in the tradition of the patristic explanation of the sacred mysteries; based as it is on the biblical images and events, it throws light on the whole economy of salvation.

The Spirit of God brooding over the waters prefigured the waters of baptism which the same Spirit is about to sanctify and so make the vehicle of his grace. In the same way the waters of the deluge showed that baptism engenders to the life of God men who were dead as a result of sin, took away the sins of the world, and were the beginning of a new life; "one and the same element was, in mystery, the end of vice and the beginning of virtues." (The Blessing of Water for Baptism, Easter Vigil Service)

In rapid succession the preface of the blessing of the water recalls the waters divided from the firmament by the Creator (Gn 1,6), the four rivers which watered the garden of Eden (Gn 2,10), the bitter water changed into sweet during the Exodus (Ex 15,23f), the water that Moses made spring from the rock (Ex 17,6); then some New Testament events associated with water: the miracle of Cana and the walking on the water. By his baptism in the Jordan Christ sanctified the water; the water and blood flowing from the side of Christ on the cross is the classic symbol of the sacraments of baptism and eucharist.

This introduction leads up to the blessing which affirms the twofold function of the baptismal bath: it is a water that purifies and that gives birth to new life. Side by side with such words as "wash," "purify," "blot out," and "heal" we see "regenerate," "renew," "re-create," "bring forth," "give birth to." "May it be a fountain that purifies, that all those who will be washed in this bath may obtain the grace of perfect purification by the action of the Holy Spirit."

This purifying power of the water of baptism not only destroys personal sins; it attacks their very source. Baptism puts off the old nature which engenders wickedness and perversity: "Here may that nature, created to the image of God and restored in the splendor of its origins, be purified from all the failures of the old nature."

During the course of the blessing the priest plunges the paschal candle into the water to signify the sanctifying descent of Christ into the waters of the Jordan. He pours in oil and chrism, in the form of the cross, to signify that the Spirit (symbolized by the oil) makes these waters his own instrument of baptismal holiness.[3]

In the early centuries the sacrament of baptism was usually given at this point in the vigil. As we said earlier, this is still the ideal time to give it. For that reason we will deal with the actual rite here.

METHODS OF ADMINISTERING BAPTISM   For many centuries baptism was by immersion, although there were exceptions. If there were no streams or pools handy, if the candidate were on his sick bed, or if there were large crowds to be baptized, water would be poured on the head.

When we speak of immersion we must not understand it as total immersion. All the evidence—the pictures and mosaics in the ancient churches and the dimensions of the baptismal pools—points to a partial immersion. The candidate stood in the water up to his knees or waist while the one who baptized him either poured the water on his head or held his head under one of the spouts which gushed water into the baptismal pool.

Because this was the usual way of administering baptism, the candidate stripped himself before going into the pool. In the East this putting off of his clothes was regarded as a symbol of putting off the "old man," of laying aside his former manner of living to embark on a completely new life. This was also the reason why the ancient rituals (St. Hippolytus', for example) pre-

[3] Modern scholars believe that these rites and the other actions which accompany the blessing of the water were introduced to act out the words of the prayer. They were devised when people no longer knew any Latin and were intended to give the people some idea of what was going on.

scribed a bath on Holy Thursday for those who would be baptized at the vigil. Of course, the proper precautions were taken to preserve modesty, either by having the women baptized separately, or even, at times, by using separate baptisteries. Those who were to be baptized laid aside not only their clothes but all ornaments, rings, pins, or anything of the sort. The women were expected to have their hair loose.

In the modern rite of baptism, immediately before the baptism proper, the candidate (or sponsor) makes the profession of faith, which is in the form of three questions:

"(Name), do you believe in God the Father Almighty, the Creator of heaven and earth?

"(Name), do you believe in Jesus Christ, his only son our Lord, who was born into this world and suffered for us?

"(Name), do you believe in the Holy Spirit; the holy Catholic Church, the communion of saints, the resurrection of the flesh, and life everlasting?"

To each of these questions the answer is "I do believe."

For centuries this was the actual formula of baptism. As the candidate made his profession of faith, the bishop poured water on his head or immersed him in the water each time. In that way there was a threefold interrogation, a threefold profession of faith in the persons of the Trinity, a threefold immersion in the water, as St. Ambrose says. (*On the Sacraments,* 2,7) This is the way baptism is described in the *Apostolic Tradition* of St. Hippolytus in A.D. 215, in St. Ambrose' treatise *On the Sacraments* over one hundred years later, and in all the ancient *ordines,* or baptismal rituals. That is why modern pastoral theologians look forward to seeing the ancient formula restored, at least for the baptism of adults, as part of the revision of all the rites demanded by the *Constitution on the Sacred Liturgy.*

The practice of threefold immersion lasted longer than the interrogation form of baptizing; baptism by infusion did not become general until the fifteenth century. In fact the Roman ritual still provides for baptism by immersion (one immersion) in those places where it is the custom; and it is the prescribed manner of baptizing in the Ambrosian rite in northern Italy.

The threefold profession of faith has been retained in the modern ritual but it takes place before the actual baptism. The sacrament is conferred by pouring the water three times on the head of the candidate while saying the words, "I baptize you in the name of the Father, and of the Son, and of the Holy Spirit."

When did this change come about and why? The "modern" form of baptism can be traced back to the eighth century and appears to have originated in the Gallican territories, approximately in what is today that part of the continent of Europe north and west of the Alps. Scholars such as Dom Thierry Maertens speculate that it probably originated in emergency baptisms. When a priest had to baptize someone in a hurry he blessed the water with a short form and baptized the candidate with the words "I baptize you. . . ." (Cf. Th. Maertens, *Histoire et Pastorale du rituel du catéchuménat*

26

et du baptême, Bruges, 1962, pp. 284f.) What began as an emergency formula in time became the normal procedure except for the solemn baptism at Easter. Gradually it came to be used at all times because by then infant baptism was the rule and the declarative form "I baptize you" appeared more natural for the baptism of infants than the interrogative form.

It must be admitted that the ancient form had its advantages. It certainly expressed more clearly that baptism is an action that involves the candidate as well as the priest. Baptism clearly appeared as a personal action, a pact concluded between the Church and the candidate. The present formula suffers from the disadvantage of making the candidate seem passive in the very act of baptism.

What happened at the moment of baptism? St. Cyril of Jerusalem says:

> Then you were led to the holy pool of divine baptism as Christ taken down from the cross was laid in the tomb already prepared. Each one was questioned in the name of the Father and of the Son and of the Holy Spirit. You made the profession of salvation and you were plunged into the water three times and came forth, signifying Christ's burial for three days. *By this action you died and you were born* and the saving water was for you at once a grave and the womb of a mother. (Lecture 20, *On the Mysteries 2, 4*)

Cyril's words are clear enough. He wants to show that the baptismal rite is an image, a picture in symbolic form of the death and resurrection. By undergoing that rite we act out mystically or sacramentally in ourselves the death and resurrection of Christ. The rite itself is a symbol that contains the reality of salvation. The reality is there but it is distinct from the symbol. By submitting to the rite we attain to the reality it symbolizes. This is important to the theology of the sacraments in general.

Baptism is an effective symbol of the death and resurrection of Christ. It does what it signifies. It represents the saving events in a corporeal way and at the same time actualizes them spiritually.

ANOINTING WITH CHRISM; WHITE GARMENTS; LIGHTED CANDLE   Immediately after the baptism the priest anoints the top of the head with holy chrism, saying as he does so: "May Almighty God, the Father of our Lord Jesus Christ, who has given you a new birth by water and the Holy Spirit and who gave you forgiveness of all your sins, himself consecrate you with the chrism of salvation in the same Jesus Christ our Lord unto eternal life. Amen."

The chrism is a mixture of olive oil and balm consecrated by the bishop on Holy Thursday. Anointing with chrism shows one of the principal effects of the baptism that has just taken place: it identifies us with Christ. The chrism itself symbolizes Christ and his own anointing with the Spirit at his baptism.

This unction recalls in particular the anointing received in biblical

27

times by kings and priests, which prefigured the anointing of Christ as priest and king. By the spiritual anointing we receive from Christ in baptism we become ourselves kings and priests, that is, sharers in his royal and priestly dignity, "members of Christ, eternal priest and king" as St. Isidore of Seville says. We are incorporated into that "chosen race" and "royal priesthood" that St. Peter speaks of.

White garments were in the early Church a symbol of heavenly glory, in particular the glory that clothed the martyrs after death. The Apocalypse describes the martyrs as "clad in white robes, bearing palms in their hands," the symbol of victory. In the *Passion of Perpetua and Felicitas,* a third-century document, Perpetua sees the martyrs who have gone before her into paradise clothed in white; this may also be an allusion to the baptismal robes.

This early symbolism justifies our seeing an eschatological meaning as well in the baptismal robes. They prefigure the future glory that is anticipated in this life, for even now baptism makes us fellow citizens with the saints. Even now we are come to Mount Zion and to the city of the living God, the heavenly Jerusalem. Here on earth we walk in the city whose light is the Lamb.

In its present form, at least, the giving of the lighted candle to the newly baptized was a late addition to the baptismal rite (eleventh-century France). The remote origin of this practice was probably the custom in some places of lighting the candles of the neophytes at the end of the Easter vigil.

Like the baptismal robe the lighted candle has an eschatological significance which we can see in the formula that goes with it: "Take this lighted candle and preserve your baptism blamelessly. Keep the commandments of God so that when the Lord shall come to the wedding feast you may go forth to meet him with all the saints in the halls of heaven and live forever and ever. Amen." This is a clear reference to the passage in the gospel where our Lord tells us to have burning lamps in our hands like men who wait for their Lord when he shall return from the wedding feast. The wedding feast is a well known biblical term for the last days. The baptized are to spend their whole lives waiting for the final coming of the Lord.

THE MASS OF THE EASTER VIGIL   After examining the rite of baptism in its historical setting and seeing that it came on Easter night as the climax of a long series of introductory rites, we can better appreciate the baptismal character of the Mass of the Easter vigil. We can understand now that it is not only the climax of the whole vigil but the completion of the baptismal rite as well. Most of the texts of this Mass refer or allude to baptism; they presume that baptism has just taken place.

The collect, for example, prays that God will preserve in the new children of his family the spirit of adoption that he has given them, and that renewed in body and spirit they may accomplish sincerely their duties as Christians.

Baptism implies changing one's life. The newly baptized Christian should show by the holiness of his life that he is a member of Christ and already a citizen of heaven. The epistle is addressed first of all to the newly baptized, then to all of us, for we are a baptized people. "If you be risen with Christ, seek the things that are above, where Christ is seated at the right hand of God. Mind the things that are above, not the things that are upon the earth. For you are dead and your life is hidden with Christ in God." (Col 3,1ff)

Alleluia is the great Easter song of the Church. It expresses the joy of the resurrection. Christ's resurrection becomes ours through baptism.

The gospel proclaims the resurrection which is the source of the new birth in the waters of baptism.

The prayer over the gifts also alludes to baptism, for it asks that the sacrifice inaugurated by the paschal mystery may be an eternal remedy for us. The paschal mystery of the death and resurrection of our Lord is the source of the eucharistic sacrifice. We are incorporated into that same mystery by baptism.

The preface shows that the whole Easter vigil is the celebration of the entire paschal mystery: the death and the resurrection of Christ. This paschal mystery is first celebrated and re-enacted in baptism. But baptism itself equips us to take part in the eucharist, the full celebration of that paschal mystery.

THE WEEK OF THE WHITE ROBES   The Easter octave is in reality the prolongation of the Easter feast itself, the joyful counterpart of Holy Week. In the early Church those who had been baptized on Easter eve continued to wear their baptismal robes during this octave and so prolonged the celebration of their baptism until Easter Saturday.

Each day during this week the neophytes took part in the special celebrations of the eucharist that were held in the stational churches of Rome. Because these Masses were proper to the feast and the season they formed a prolonged contemplation of the whole mystery of Christ, the paschal mystery, and consequently of the mystery of Christian initiation which introduces us into the paschal mystery. The texts of these Masses form a wonderful catechesis of baptism, confirmation, and the eucharist.

TYPOLOGY OF BAPTISM: OLD TESTAMENT
CROSSING OF THE RED SEA

The crossing of the Red Sea and baptism stand in close relationship to each other. What was prefigured in the one was accomplished in the other The Israelites under the leadership of Moses, who was himself the instrument of God, crossed through the miraculously divided Red Sea. No sooner had they passed than the armies of Pharao followed them into the pathway, only to be overwhelmed and destroyed by the waters. Here we meet again the theme of the waters of judgment and destruction. This event was a turning point in Israel's history. It marked the birth of this people to freedom and liberty.

That the crossing of the Red Sea is a type of baptism (and an important one) appears in one of the earliest New Testament documents, the first epistle of St. Paul to the Corinthians: "I want you all to know, brethren, that our fathers were all under the cloud, and all passed through the sea, and all were baptized into Moses in the cloud and in the sea, and all ate of the same supernatural food and all drank the same supernatural drink." (1 Cor 10,2-6) Then he says that "all these things were done to us in figure." (1 Cor 10,6) It is not clear whether he means "figure" in the sense of "type" or of "warning": "These things are a warning to us." In any case the use of the term "baptized" in connection with the Old Testament event is significant.

But if there is some ambiguity about St. Paul's interpretation of the crossing of the Red Sea there is none about the interpretation of the Fathers. One after another, in East and West, they see it as the image of baptism because they see it as the type of the redemption. Thus Tertullian in the West writes in his treatise *On Baptism:*

> When the people, willingly leaving Egypt, escaped from the power of the Egyptian king by passing over the water, the water destroyed the king and all his army. *What could be a clearer figure of baptism?* The peoples are delivered from the world, and this is done by the water, and they leave behind the devil who has hitherto tyrannized over them, destroyed in the water.

The early Church viewed redemption as a conflict with the demon in which Christ was the victor. By this victory humanity was released from Satan's power and set free. This victory and the liberation it brought, the early Church believed, was applied to every Christian in the sacrament of baptism. Such, indeed, is what the early writers mean by the "mystery" of baptism. The victory won once for all nevertheless takes place again *"in mysterio,"* sacramentally. Once again in baptism the demon is conquered and man is saved. The redemptive event is extended to the individual Christian, who has already been redeemed in principle.

The connection between the Exodus event and baptism, in the mind of the Fathers, is this: what God did then to deliver a people from a material tyrant, he now accomplishes by the sacrament of water to deliver a spiritual people from a tyrant over their spiritual well-being. Water once accomplished a physical or material passage and ensured its success; now again water accomplishes a passage, this time a spiritual one.

Through his death and burial Christ, himself the new Israel, made the painful journey back to his Father. Like his fathers and ours he passed through the Red Sea (of his blood) to come out on the other side through the resurrection. By that resurrection he ended his journey back to the

Father. The process by which we make our journey back to the Father means that we relive in ourselves the drama of Christ's return. We do this through baptism. In this way the pasch of Christ becomes the pasch of Christians. Baptism is our passover.

The reason why baptism is the Christian's pasch, his new birth, is that in this sacrament the pasch of Christ, his death and resurrection, becomes operative in us under the symbol of the water. Baptism is a sacrament that effectively images or re-presents the death and resurrection of Christ. This is why the *Exsultet* on Easter night places the three events side by side: the Old Testament prefigurement, the New Testament fulfillment, the sacrament.

> This is the paschal solemnity in which that true Lamb was slain by whose blood the doorposts of the faithful are hallowed.
>
> This is the night in which you first caused our forefathers, the children of Israel to pass through the Red Sea with dry feet, when escaping from Egypt (Exodus). . . .
>
> This is the night which now throughout the world restores to grace and unity and sanctity those that believe in Christ (baptism). . . .
>
> This is the night in which Christ rose victorious from the grave after destroying the bonds of death (the resurrection). . . .

NEW TESTAMENT THEOLOGY OF BAPTISM

Baptism in St. Paul

The teaching of St. Paul on baptism is in many ways the most complete baptismal teaching of the New Testament. Even when he is not directly referring to it, the allusions that he makes indicate that baptism is almost always present to his mind. An analysis of the Pauline baptismal texts must, therefore, always form the greater part of any New Testament study of the meaning of baptism.

The whole of this doctrine hinges around the idea of incorporation into Christ. Because the baptized person has been inserted into the death and resurrection of Christ he is in a new state, a new condition; he walks in newness of life and is a new creature. The classical expression of this teaching is found in the sixth chapter of the Epistle to the Romans. Indeed we may say that all references to baptism in St. Paul's writings are only an unfolding of the consequences of what this chapter teaches. That is why it is so important to examine every line and word of this passage.[4]

Romans 6,3ff is the crucial passage of St. Paul's writings on the subject of baptism as associating the believer in the death and resurrection of Christ.

[4] We should note that Paul sometimes uses the word "baptism" to describe not only the sacrament of the water itself, but the whole process of Christian initiation.

Just before he reaches this point, he has been telling the Roman Christians (who were nearly all Jews at the time) that because of the obedience of one Man we are acquitted of the sin of Adam. Where once sin held sway, now God's favor reigns through his gift of righteousness and eternal life bestowed on us through Christ. The thought then occurs to Paul that some misguided souls might think that he was encouraging sin so as to obtain an even greater triumph of God's mercy. He answers this objection by showing that the Christian has been freed from sin by the death of Christ and so should not come under its sway again.

> For how shall we who are dead to sin still live in it? Do you not know that all we who have been baptized into Christ Jesus have been baptized into his death? For we were buried with him by means of baptism into death, in order that just as Christ has risen from the dead through the glory of the Father, so we also may walk in newness of life. For if we have been united with him in the likeness of his death, we shall be so in the likeness of his resurrection also. For we know that our old self has been crucified with him, in order that the body of sin may be destroyed, that we may no longer be slaves to sin, for he who is dead is acquitted of sin. But if we have died with Christ we believe that we shall also live together with Christ, for we know that Christ having risen from the dead dies now no more; death shall no longer have dominion over him. For the death that he died, he died to sin once for all, but the life he lives he lives to God. Thus do you consider yourselves as dead to sin but alive to God in Christ Jesus.

The whole point of the passage is that baptism is an effective image (or sign) of the death and resurrection of Christ. By undergoing this rite the believer dies with Christ as though he himself had died with him upon the cross. The experience of the head becomes the experience of the members. Baptism is an immersion into his death, that is, a sharing in it and in its effects. The death the believer undergoes is a real death but not a physical one. He does not die physically, because his soul is not separated from his body. What, then, happens? He dies to sin, to lower nature. By the physical act of washing accompanied by the word he is joined to the body-person of Christ in the moment of his death. The death of Christ was a death to sin first of all because it was the complete surrender of self, and sin is essentially selfishness.

In the rite of baptism, the candidate is buried in the water, drowned in it. This symbolism remains even today, from the fact that the candidate's head (which stands for the whole body) is covered with water. Whether we use a little or a great deal of water does not really matter; the sign is there and it is a sign of death (for burial follows death). Buried beneath the waters the Christian dies to the world. Baptism marks the end of his world. St. Paul reasons: How can you continue to live a worldly and sinful life?

You are dead to all that. You said goodbye to it when you went down into the waters of baptism. "How shall we who are dead to sin still live in it?" (Rom 6,2)

By entering the water the catechumen enters with Christ into the tomb and disappears from the eyes of the world together with Christ. "You are dead and your life is hidden with Christ in God," St. Paul says in Colossians 3,3. He is united with Christ, *identified* with him, inserted into the Christ of the cross and of the tomb. This means that he makes his own the sacrifice of Christ and enters into the dispositions and sentiments that Christ had at the moment of his death. "Let that mind be in you which was also in Christ Jesus, who humbled himself, becoming obedient unto death, even the death of the cross." (Phil 2,8) This, incidentally, is the reason why the baptized becomes a priest (in the New Testament sense of the word). He makes himself with Christ "a victim, living, holy, pleasing to God." (Rom 12,1) The baptized Christian becomes *personally* involved in the sacrifice of Christ. Through the medium of this water and the word and the power of the Holy Spirit he is at one with him. He is taken up into the one, unique, perfect sacrifice so that he can say "I live, now not I, but Christ lives in me," the Christ of Calvary, the self-giving, self-sacrificing Christ. The old self comes to an end through baptismal death.

But this is only half the story of the full reality. The death that we undergo at baptism is simultaneously the end of the old self and the beginning of the new. For we are not engrafted into the dead corpse of Christ but joined to one who came forth gloriously from the tomb. His death was a victorious death, a life-giving death. "Christ having risen from the dead dies now no more, death shall no longer have dominion over him." (Rom 6,9) Through his resurrection he entered upon a new life. Since the Christian repeats Christ's experience, the same thing happens to him: he simultaneously partakes of the death and the resurrection. He has a risen life, the life of the Son of God in the flesh. He walks in newness of life. Baptism is a death and a rebirth at the same time; a death because it is a rebirth and a rebirth because it is a death.

Just as the Savior came forth alive from the tomb the conqueror of death and hell, so the Christian is born to victory in the font of baptism. For this reason the blessing of the water at Easter calls the font the womb of Mother Church where we are born anew to the life of grace. For this reason too the sacrament is called the sacrament of regeneration. By it the catechumen is supernaturally regenerated, that is, he begins to live the life of the Son of God and becomes a sharer in the life of the blessed Trinity.

Here is where the doctrine of St. Paul and the doctrine of St. John, though differing in emphasis, show that they are basically the same. John considers the sacrament as a new birth by water and the Holy Spirit; for Paul it is incorporation into Christ and identification with him. But incorporation into Christ is incorporation into the risen humanity of the Lord, into that body that was glorified by the Holy Spirit. So baptism for St. Paul, *33* as for St. John, is simply a birth into newness of life. "If any man is in Christ, he is a new creature." (2 Cor 5,17)

Now we have the whole picture. The sacrament of baptism immerses the catechumen, plunges him in the death and resurrection of the Savior and causes him to participate in both, to make them his own. The rest of his life as a Christian is only a carrying on of this initial event. This is why the sacrament is not repeated; one can be born again supernaturally only once. But one can and must carry out the implications of that once-for-all event. One must continue to reproduce the mystery of the death and resurrection, says St. Paul in another place, "that the rising also of Jesus may be manifested in us." (2 Cor 4,10)

Celebration of the Lord's pasch, his passage from death to life, unites us to his crucifixion, resurrection, and glorification—the whole paschal mystery at once. The paschal mystery becomes our mystery. St. Paul expresses this identification with Christ in many ways, perhaps never more effectively than in the passage from the letter to the Ephesians, "But God who is rich in mercy, by reason of his very great love wherewith he has loved us even when we were dead by reason of our sins, brought us to life *together with* Christ (by grace you have been saved) and raised us up *together with* Christ, and enthroned us *together with him* in the heavenly realms." (Eph 2,4ff) The Greek is clearer than the English translation here. By using a series of verbs compounded with *syn* (the Greek for "with") Paul shows that we share together with Christ the experience of his crucifixion and exaltation. "He who cleaves to the Lord is one spirit with him." (1 Cor 6,17)

This identification does not mean that there is any fusion or confusion of the person of Christ with ours. Neither is our individuality absorbed by his, so that we cease to be ourselves. What this does mean is that we become intimately united to him so that his thoughts become our thoughts, his actions our actions. He lives and acts in us.

St. Paul gives a large place in his writings to the idea that because baptism identifies us with Christ it makes us the sons of God. This is of course closely related to the themes of rebirth and the new creation. To be born again, to walk in newness of life, is to become by grace something of what Jesus is. "But when the fullness of time came, God sent his son born of a woman, born under the law, that we might receive the adoption of sons. And because you are sons God has sent the spirit of his Son into our hearts, crying 'Abba,' Father. So that he is no longer a slave but a son and if a son, an heir also through God." (Gal 4,4-7) The apostle does not mention baptism directly in this passage but everything that he says supposes baptism and of course it must be read in the light of his other teaching on baptism.

St. Paul in fact gives this adoption of sons as the very central object of the whole plan of redemption when he says in the Epistle to the Ephesians: "He predestined us to be adopted through Jesus Christ as his sons, according to the purpose of his will, unto the praise of the glory of his grace, with which he has favored us in his beloved Son." (Eph 1,5f) This was the mystery hidden from all ages, revealed now in these last times, which St. Paul was specially committed to proclaim to the Gentiles. Again he does not speak here specifically of baptism but he uses the formula "in Christ Jesus" which has baptismal overtones. In the eyes of Paul redemption means a reconstituted humanity, and that reconstituted humanity, that new creation, is Christ. We must be incorporated into that new humanity. The means of incorporation, as is apparent all through his writings, is the bath of regeneration, baptism.

> But when the goodness and kindness of God our savior appeared, then not by reason of good works that we did ourselves but according to his mercy, he saved us through the *bath of regeneration* and *renewal* by the Holy Spirit, *whom he has abundantly poured out upon us through* Jesus Christ our savior, in order that justified by his grace, we may be heirs in the hope of life everlasting. (Ti 3,4ff)

This passage is valuable not only because it refers to baptism, the bath of regeneration (rebirth), but also because it shows that in the mind of the writer the sacrament *itself* saves and justifies us.

It is significant too that he speaks of the *outpouring* of the Spirit, water being the traditional symbol of the Spirit. By using this term in connection with the reference to the bath he brings out the relationship between the pouring of the water and the outpouring of the Spirit.

BAPTISM AS ENLIGHTENMENT   Although St. Paul nowhere directly refers to baptism as an enlightenment, he does make several allusions to enlightenment and light. When we remember that baptism was called "enlightenment" in the early Church, probably even in apostolic times, his use of these expressions is significant. They must be taken into account in any survey of his teaching.

They all occur in the Epistle to the Ephesians, a fact significant in itself because of the baptismal overtones of this epistle. "For once you were darkness, now you are light in the Lord; walk as children of the light, for the fruit of the light is found in all that is good and right and true." (Eph 5,8ff)

This passage comes in a context where Paul has been speaking of the works of darkness, such things as immorality and impurity and covetousness. No one who does these things will have any inheritance in the kingdom of God. It is hard to escape the conclusion, therefore, that Ephesians 5 contains a reference to the concrete experience of having received the light in baptism, of having been joined to him who is the light of the world.

This appears all the more likely, if not certain, when we look at the verses which occur a little later in the same chapter. Exegetes consider in fact that they may be a fragment of an early Christian baptismal hymn: "Awake, sleeper, and arise from the dead and Christ shall give you light."

35

(Eph 5,14) Paul's joining of this remark about Christ giving light to a reference to rising from the dead is especially interesting in view of his known teaching that baptism joins us to the risen Christ. "To be enlightened" in the Bible is often a synonym for "to be saved." Since we are saved in the concrete by being joined to the saving acts of Christ in baptism, the baptismal reference in this passage can hardly be denied.

BAPTISM AS INCORPORATION INTO THE CHURCH   Another representative passage in St. Paul is 1 Cor 12,13: "For by one spirit we were all baptized into one body—Jews or Greeks, slaves or free—and all were made to drink of one spirit." Here he teaches that baptism is the means of incorporation into the Christian community, which is the body of Christ. This incorporation is the work of the Spirit. This passage must be considered together with the passage from Romans spoken of earlier, in which Paul makes it clear that baptism incorporates us into the Church because it incorporates us into the Lord of the Church at the moment of his death and resurrection.

It also must be considered along with the better known passage in Ephesians 4,1–6 in which he lays special stress on the relation between baptism and Christian unity:

> I, therefore, a prisoner for the Lord, beg you to lead a life worthy of the calling to which you have been called . . . eager to maintain the unity of the spirit in the bond of peace. There is one body and one spirit, just as you were called to the one hope that belongs to your call; one Lord, one faith, one baptism, one God and father of all, who is above all, and through all and in all.

Baptism is what joins us to the one body of Christ and so unites us in the bond of peace.

In fact Paul's teaching on baptism is so closely related to his teaching on the Church that they appear as aspects of the one doctrine; it is almost impossible to separate them. For him the whole meaning of baptism lies precisely in the fact that it is the means of incorporation into Christ and the Church, which are the same. Baptism is entrance into the new people of God, the reconstituted Israel, the household and family of God. It changes us from strangers and aliens, makes us "fellow citizens of the saints, and members of God's household." (Eph 2,19f)

We usually think of baptism as, first of all, the sacrament that cleanses from sin, original or actual; we are less likely to consider the other aspects that St. Paul emphasizes. This does not mean that he neglected the purifying work of baptism. In fact he refers to it directly and indirectly in several places. He also adds the fact that it sanctifies and justifies as well as cleanses.

In the First Epistle to the Corinthians, after making a long litany of the criminals and sinners who emphatically will not inherit the kingdom of God, he says bluntly enough: "And such were some of you. But you were washed, were sanctified, were justified in the name of the Lord Jesus Christ and in the Spirit of our God." (1 Cor 6,11) This is a clear reference to baptism; we can almost hear the echo of the invocation of the Holy Trinity used in the baptismal rite.

We can see this even more clearly if we place other passages alongside it, like the glorious one in Ephesians 5,25–28:

> Husbands, love your wives as Christ loved the Church and gave himself up for her, that he might sanctify her, having cleansed her by washing of water with the word, that he might present the Church to himself in splendor without spot or wrinkle of any such thing, that she might be holy and without blemish.

The rite of baptism, therefore, according to St. Paul's teaching, cleanses, purifies, washes away sin, restores to life and health, sanctifies, and justifies.

But what about faith? Does he not insist that we are justified by faith? Why then is baptism necessary? Since we cannot discuss this extremely complicated doctrine in detail here, suffice it to say that for Paul faith and baptism are so closely bound together that it is impossible to separate them. Baptism demands faith and faith is crowned by baptism. For the apostle as for the Catholic Church at all times, faith and baptism are but the outside and inside of the same reality.

Baptism in St. John

According to many modern exegetes and commentators John's chief purpose in writing his gospel was to show that the life of Jesus was continued in the Church chiefly through the sacraments of baptism and the eucharist. Through these sacraments, when they are approached in faith, we are able to enter into life-giving contact with the glorified humanity of Christ. This contact results in our new birth as God's sons: "But to all who received him [that is, came in contact with him through faith] he gave the power to become the sons of God, to those who believed in his name . . . who were born not of the will of men but of the will of God." (Jn 1,12f)

Because of this purpose these two sacraments seem never to be far from the mind of the evangelist. This is why we can say that besides the explicit reference to baptism in such passages as the discourse with Nicodemus: "Unless a man is born again of water and the Holy Spirit . . ." there are many indirect references which yield their meaning only in the light of the entire gospel. This conversation shows that baptism is a new birth. "Truly, truly I say to you, unless one is born anew, he cannot see the kingdom of God. That which is born of the flesh is flesh and that which is born of the spirit is spirit." (Jn 3,5f) This must be understood in the light of all the other related New Testament passages, especially those in the fourth gospel itself. "To those who received him he gave the power to be sons of God." (Jn 1,12)

37

Baptism makes us the sons of God because it is a new birth to the life of God.

Another important baptismal reference in St. John, which is at the same time a reference to the Holy Spirit, is that spoken by Jesus at the feast of tabernacles:

> If any one thirst let him come to me and drink. He who believes in me, as the scripture has said, "Out of his heart shall flow rivers of living water." Now this he said about the Spirit, which those who believed in him were to receive; for as yet the Spirit had not been given because Jesus was not yet glorified. (Jn 7,37ff)

This passage is rich in meaning. The image of coming to Christ and slaking one's thirst from the fountains of water that flow from his heart (for that is the more probable interpretation of this somewhat confused text) suggests baptism. The Fathers of the Church saw in the water and blood coming from his side the emblems of the sacraments of baptism and the eucharist. The one who believes in him, that is, who adheres to him by faith, will experience the outpouring of the Spirit. Once again the Spirit is directly associated with water. And if we remember that in the early Church believing was concretely expressed by receiving baptism, the baptismal character of the whole passage becomes even more clear.

But its center is the promise of the Holy Spirit in the image of streams of living water. "This he said of the Spirit which had not yet been given because Jesus was not yet glorified." Water in abundance was to be one of the signs of the messianic times. In the eyes of the prophets this water, springing up or poured out, was an image of the Spirit of Yahweh. "I will pour out waters upon the thirsty ground . . . I will pour out my Spirit upon your seed." (Is 44,3) This outpouring of the Spirit has a necessary connection with the glorification of Christ (that is, his death and resurrection). The source of Spirit is the glorified body of Christ: "The Spirit had not yet been given because Jesus had not yet been glorified." (Jn 7,39) This passage must be placed side by side with Romans 6,4–11, which it complements and illuminates. Through contact with the blessed passion and glorious resurrection of Christ the neophyte receives the spirit of adoption. He is born again to the life of grace, the life of the Spirit. He drinks from the torrent of living water (the Spirit) which flows from the side of Christ.

There is indeed an intimate connection between the death and resurrection of Christ and that outpouring of the Spirit which is the climax and goal of the whole redeeming work. The Spirit is the heavenly Spirit who comes down from the bosom of God. He can be sent only from on high and therefore only from one who is himself on high. Since the whole sanctifying work of Christ consists of sending the Spirit, it was necessary for Christ to be exalted to the right hand of the Father before he could fully accomplish his work. He had to be raised up in his flesh to the glory of the Father. But he could be glorified only by passing through death. Christ's glorious body is, consequently, the only point of contact the believer has with the Holy Spirit. The Spirit can come to us only through that body. We, in turn, can come in contact with it only through the holy mysteries, baptism and the eucharist. This is why "believing" in Christ necessarily means receiving the sacraments.

The favorite symbol of baptism in the early Church was the story of the man born blind, in the ninth chapter of St. John's gospel. With singular unanimity all see in this story an emblem or image of the great effect of the sacrament: enlightenment. The story occupied a large place in the iconography as well as the catechesis of the primitive Church. This scene from the gospel was depicted everywhere. The passage that narrates it was read in Rome in the Mass of the great *scrutinium* in preparation for baptism.

The whole narrative is a baptismal catechesis, intended to instruct the people of the evangelist's time that baptism is enlightenment. Enlightenment consists of faith. Faith is spiritual vision enabling us to see things as God sees them, with their proper value and in the right perspective. Baptism is the sacrament that bestows faith as well as puts the seal upon faith. Faith fully understood not only makes us see the truth; it impels us to adhere to it. Faith moves the will as well as the intellect. To say that baptism is the sacrament of faith means then that it not only crowns the act of believing but it gives the power to believe more completely, that is, *to adhere to* what we believe. The man in the gospel "falling down, worshipped him," when he said "I believe, Lord." (Jn 9,38) That is, he submitted himself to Jesus. This is what baptism does, it consecrates us to the service of Christ. The baptismal overtones are even stronger in the ninth chapter of John's gospel just quoted from, for it is the opinion of many exegetes that the questions and the answers probably echo the ritual of baptism in New Testament times.

Besides the passages in his gospel, the epistles of St. John contain striking teaching about baptism. Especially noteworthy is the famous passage, "This is he who came by water and blood, Jesus Christ, not with the water only but with the water and the blood." (1 Jn 5,6) This is an allusion to the close connection between Christian baptism and the death of Christ. The entire epistle is devoted to a typical Johannine theme, birth from God. He that believes is born of God. "Whoever believes that Jesus is the Christ is born of God" (1 Jn 5,1) and so whoever is born of God overcomes the world. "Who is the conqueror of the world but he who believes that Jesus is the Son of God?" (1 Jn 5,5) and finally, "This is the victory that overcomes the world: our faith." (1 Jn 5,4) None of these texts taken by itself can be proved to be a reference to baptism. But taken in the context of the whole letter, these texts are seen to be not only references to baptism but probably echoes of the New Testament baptismal ritual. For John, as we have seen, faith is not an abstract concept but a reality that takes concrete form in the sacraments of baptism and the eucharist.

Baptism in the First Epistle of St. Peter

Although not everyone accepts the thesis of some scholars, notably C. H. Dodd, that 1 Peter is a baptismal liturgy, there is little doubt that it reflects the baptismal liturgy of the first century. The first four chapters seem in fact to be a homily addressed to the newly baptized. It is filled with allusions to Old Testament types of baptism and to Old Testament events that prefigure the Christian initiation rite. The doctrine of the epistle agrees with the more developed teaching of Paul and John.

Twice, in the first chapter, Peter says that we have been born again. He attributes this new birth to the resurrection of the Lord, and more directly to the sprinkling of his blood (an obvious allusion to the baptismal rite). He says too that we have been reborn of incorruptible seed "through the word of God." This suggests the words of St. Paul quoted earlier about the invocation of the word, which has always, in one form or another, been part of the baptismal rite.

He describes the new Christians as dear children and newborn babes, and exhorts them to live in the innocence of babes.

He refers specifically to baptism in Chapter 3, saying that just as Noah was saved from the deluge by the ark "through water" so we now are saved by baptism; but "baptism saves us through the resurrection of Jesus Christ." (1 Pt 3,21) It is very interesting to see that he makes the point that it is not the mere action of washing with water that saves us—all that this can do is cleanse us from physical defilement—but the whole rite, which includes "the inquiry of a good conscience after God." Exegetes see in this a reference to those questions about the faith of the one baptized which accompanied the rite of baptism.

Perhaps the most striking teaching about baptism and what it does is that given in the second chapter, where the writer shows that as a result of baptism the Christian becomes a living stone built into the temple of God, a member of a priestly community consecrated to God's service and worship, one of God's own people.

THE EFFECTS OF BAPTISM

What does baptism do? We have seen what the Scriptures, the Church Fathers, and the liturgy tell us about the effects of this sacrament. Now we can sum up these teachings and make a synthesis of the doctrine of the Church on baptism.

First of all, baptism cleanses from sin and remits the punishment due to sin because it applies the saving action of Christ to the baptized. It blots out all sin, original and personal if there be any. We still must suffer the temporal punishment due to sin and the consequences of original sin as well as the aftereffects of actual sin. But in the divine plan these very sufferings become a means to glory through union with Christ. They are part of the redemptive plan, the means of carrying out our baptismal commitment.

Baptism does more than cleanse us from sin—it makes us pleasing to God because of its justifying power. This justification is a new birth to sonship, to the life of divine grace and favor. The new birth is achieved by the indwelling of the Holy Spirit, the sanctifier. By natural birth we are made capable of divine acts. This, incidentally, is the justification for the practice of baptizing infants. There is as much reason, and more, for bringing them to new birth as there is for bringing them into the world in the first place. The gift of life is great, but the gift of divine life is greater still.

Baptism is a bath that regenerates and cleanses because it incorporates us into Christ. The baptized is "in Christ," that is, he lives with his life. At the same time he is "in the Spirit" because the Spirit dwells in him and makes him live the life of Christ.

Because it incorporates a man into Christ, baptism at the same time incorporates him into the Church which is the body of Christ. Baptism incorporates us into a royal and priestly people, makes us the members of a worshiping community. It "deputes us to worship," as St. Thomas says. This it does by the character impressed upon us in baptism. "Character" is the word that theologians have chosen to designate the Greek word *"sphragis"* (seal, impress, likeness) of which St. Paul speaks. The character is an indelible and distinctive mark that impresses upon the baptized a participation in the priesthood of Christ. It is an image, a likeness of Christ the priest, that gives us the power to do priestly acts. It consecrates us and sets us aside for worship. More specifically it associates us with Christ's own perfect worship of his heavenly Father. Some theologians stress that the baptized is made a member of Christ *because* he is made a member of the Church. This is only to say that the Church is the assembly of those whose work is the praise of God under the headship of Christ, "in union of the Holy Spirit."

The external rite that imparts the priestly character of Christ is the rite of admission into the *"plebs sancta,"* the community of the faithful. The very term "faithful" traditionally designates those who have received baptism. Only those who are validly baptized can be considered as belonging to the faithful.

To express it in the traditional language of theologians, the effects of baptism are character and grace. These are not separate effects, however, for the character brings grace with it and so completes the likeness of Christ in the one baptized.

THE SUBJECT OF BAPTISM

"God wills that all men be saved and come to the knowledge of the truth." (1 Tim 2,4) This means that all men must be baptized: we can be saved only by communion in the death and resurrection of Christ, and we come into contact with this saving act only by baptism. Christianity is not a doctrine or a code of ethics; it is above all a life, the life of Christ in us, and that life cannot come to us by our merely willing it.

The necessity of submitting to baptism is based ultimately on the incarnation. God has arranged that salvation come to us in the touch of a hand, the sound of a human voice. Just as the salvation of the world was worked out in the sacred humanity of our Lord, so our individual salvation can be accomplished only through those material elements that prolong the sacred humanity in another mode.

Without the actual reception of baptism—or at least the desire for reception (for those who cannot, for one reason or other, receive it in fact)—we cannot be saved. "He that believes and is baptized will be saved," said the Lord; "he that believes not shall be condemned." (Mk 16,16) Not only must all men be baptized, they should be baptized *without delay* so as not to impede the work of salvation in any way. The law of the Church stipulates that infants should be baptized as soon as possible and there is a grave obligation upon parents in this matter (Canon 770). Delay should not go beyond a few days, not only because of the danger of the child's dying without baptism but also that the seed of Christian life may be planted in the child and thereby have its earliest effect.

For adults it is a different matter. They should be baptized only after they have been thoroughly instructed and prepared, and have given sufficient proof of their good dispositions. Even then the law of the Church requires that, if it is convenient, the baptism of adults be postponed until the Easter vigil (Canon 772).

Baptism is not a magic rite but a personal meeting between Christ and the one baptized. To receive it validly one must have the intention of being baptized and the proper faith. To receive it with profit one must be converted from his sinful ways and be willing to renounce Satan and adhere to Christ. It is impossible to start a new life without abandoning the old one or to be purified without having the desire to be cleansed of one's sins. This conversion is expressed by the renouncing of Satan and all his works and pomps and, in general, by submitting to the entire rite. One who has never been baptized does not need to make a confession of sins, or to do any acts of penance. But those who are conditionally baptized do have to make a confession of sins.

The faith that is required for baptism is belief in Christ as the Savior and in the teaching of Christ as it is preserved in the Church and expressed in the Apostles' Creed. Especially it demands belief in the Trinity and the incarnation. Anyone who does not believe in these things can hardly be baptized, for baptism is the act of professing the faith in a concrete way. On the other hand, baptism increases this faith in us and makes it a lively faith, a faith that works through charity and expresses itself in commitment to Christ. This commitment can and should be developed and deepened through the years. Baptism is a dynamic action that in one sense is always being continued. When St. Paul speaks of "justifying faith" it is this kind of which he speaks. Mere intellectual assent to the truth is not enough to save us, though it would enable us to receive baptism validly.

Since baptism is the sacrament of faith and presupposes conversion in him who petitions it, how can infants be baptized when they cannot even ask for it? This question has led many to reject infant baptism and to defer it until such time as the person is old enough to profess his faith of his own free will. It is hard to *prove* the necessity of infant baptism from the Scriptures; nevertheless there are indications that such has always been the practice of the Church. Some exegetes think that the saying of Jesus about "letting the little children come to me and forbidding them not" was included in the gospel narrative to teach that this practice is not only lawful but desirable. Whether that is so or not, there can be no doubt that it expresses the instinctive feeling of the Church in the matter.

THE MINISTER OF BAPTISM

Baptism is a ministerial rite. That is, it is not something that one can do for himself; someone must do it for him. No one can baptize himself validly for the simple reason that it is the rite that admits one into the Church of Christ and you cannot admit yourself into any society. That has to be done by the society itself through its lawful representatives.

Normally the lawful representative of that society which is the Catholic Church is the local head of the community, the Catholic bishop of the area, who in turn represents Christ, the true minister of all the sacraments. Anyone else who baptizes is acting as the bishop's deputy, though priests and deacons act by a different title than lay people. In ancient times, as we have seen, the bishop either did the baptizing himself or at least presided over the baptism. The idea was that the father of the Christian community should beget new spiritual children through this sign.

Since baptism is no longer confined to one or two nights of the year (it now being physically impossible for the bishop to be present at all baptisms, let alone perform them himself), the parish priest or his assistant has become the ordinary minister of this sacrament. Deacons also may administer solemn baptism with the permission of the pastor. No one else not in holy orders can celebrate the full rite of baptism.

In case of necessity anyone, man or woman, even though not a Catholic, can validly baptize. All that is necessary is that he have the intention of doing what the Church does and do it correctly, pouring water on the head so that it washes the skin of the head and at the same time saying the words, "I baptize you in the name of the Father, and of the Son, and of the Holy Spirit." This layman becomes, for the time being, the representative of the Church and the deputy of the local bishop. The Church allows this departure from

43

normal procedure so that the dying person may not be deprived of the blessings of the sacrament. But if the person recovers, the other rites must be supplied, and if there is any doubt about the validity, the person must be baptized conditionally.

CHILDREN
WHO DIE WITHOUT BAPTISM

A book of this kind is hardly the place to enter into any great detail regarding the fate of those children who die without baptism. Theologians have discussed the problem for centuries, but in many ways it is an insoluble one. All that we know is that baptism is necessary for salvation, and on the other hand that God wills that all men be saved. Therefore theologians since Augustine's time have postulated a place of natural happiness called limbo (Latin, "edge, border"), where the souls of those infants excluded from the vision of God because they died without baptism exist eternally.

The difficulty about this solution is that there is no teaching of the Church on the subject to substantiate it except the one which says that baptism is necessary for salvation. The rest is only speculation. The chief objection to this solution is its legalism which depicts God as bound by his own sacraments, whereas we know that he is not.

Once again, baptism is necessary for salvation because it is the only means we know of to incorporate us into Christ. But God surely has other ways of achieving that end. We might even argue that if the faith of the Church can supply for the faith of the child in infant baptism, why should not the desire of the Church supply for at least a baptism of desire in those infants who are deprived of baptism of water through carelessness or ignorance?

BAPTISM
AS A WAY OF CHRISTIAN LIFE

Christian spirituality is a baptismal spirituality; the Christian life is nothing else than a living out of the implications of our baptism. "If you are risen with Christ seek the things that are above. Mind the things that are above, not the things that are below. For you are dead and your life is hidden with Christ in God. When Christ, who is your life, shall appear then you also will appear with him in glory." (Col 3,1–4) "You were once darkness, now you are light in the Lord. Walk then as children of the light." (Eph 5,7f)

As a result of baptism our whole situation is changed. We live in a new world and breathe a new and purer air. The life principle of that new existence is the Spirit of God. "They that are led by the Spirit of God are the sons of God." (Rom 8,14) Baptism marks a definite break with one's former manner of living. It is a turning back upon one's old life, a death to sin and lower nature and a simultaneous rising to a new life lived under the power of the Spirit of God. It is setting out upon a new road, a movement and a passage toward God. It is a walking "in his steps." Each baptized Christian can say and should be able to say more and more, "I live, now not I, but Christ lives in me." (Gal 2,20)

The Christian life is a simultaneous dying and rising with Christ, the continuation in our mortal flesh of the life of the glorified Son of God, the prolongation of the incarnation. It is an identification with Christ who will —if allowed to do so—manifest himself more and more in our mortal flesh. "Our manner of living is in heaven," St. Paul says. The diligent study of Pauline spirituality will show that this means, in the concrete, that we are associated with the "spiritual sacrifice" of the heavenly High Priest himself, indeed that we reproduce that sacrifice in our own lives. "I exhort you, brethren, to present yourselves as victims, holy, living, and pleasing to God. This is your spiritual service [worship]." (Rom 12,1) The Christian life is a continued act of worship because Christ's own life is a continued worship. In this way baptism shows itself as a "mystery," a salvific event. It is not so much an action as a life that we live.

A violent wind, fire come down from heaven, God's praise on every tongue. But the Lord is not in wind or in the fire. He is in the Spirit set as a seal on the spirit of every man who receives him (Courtesy The Walters Art Gallery, Baltimore).

CHAPTER TWO

CONFIRMATION

The second stage of Christian initiation is the sacrament of confirmation. This is the sacred rite which, by the anointing with chrism and the words of the bishop, bestows the Holy Spirit in a special way upon the baptized Christian. It equips the believer to live the Christian life more perfectly and to take his rightful part in the work of the Church. Confirmation is the complement and the completion of baptism, and can be rightly understood only in relation to that sacrament. Although confirmation is a separate sacrament, it nevertheless is not *isolated*. It stands in very close relation to baptism and to the eucharist, being part of the single process of Christian initiation.

This relationship was more clearly seen in the ancient Church (as it still is in the Eastern Churches), when the newly baptized went from the font directly into the presence of the bishop, who sealed them with the seal of the Spirit. This is one reason why even today the rite of confirmation is so short in comparison to the rite of baptism; it came as the completion of the baptismal rite and in the setting of the whole Easter vigil. When in the course of time it was separated from the vigil a few prayers were added, but it still shows that it formed part of a larger, more complex rite, the whole rite of Christian initiation.

Confirmation was never seriously questioned as a sacrament until the time of the Protestant Reformation. Luther and Calvin claimed that it was of purely ecclesiastical origin and that it had no warrant in Scripture. Cranmer, too, excluded it as a sacrament but retained the rite of laying on of hands. Some modern Anglicans regard it as a sacrament in the full sense of the word, but not in the same class with baptism. Others regard it as a secondary sacrament.

Because the reformers denied that it was a sacrament, the Council of Trent was compelled to define it as one of the seven sacraments of the new law and more specifically to say:

> If anyone says that the confirmation of those who have been baptized is an idle ceremony and not rather a true and proper sacrament, or that of old it was nothing more than a kind of catechism whereby they who were near adolescence gave an account of their faith in the presence of the Church, let him be condemned. (Session 7, *On Confirmation,* Canon 1)

It is therefore of divine faith that confirmation is a sacrament, that is, an outward sign of invisible grace, and that it produces this grace of itself. The words "true and proper" remove any doubt or ambiguity on the subject.

But if the sacramental character of the rite is defined, there is no definition of the "matter" and "form" or the effects of the sacrament. This does not mean that there is no teaching on the subject; it simply means that the Church has never formally defined anything. (Much of the teaching of the Church has never been formally defined, for that matter.)

The greatest part of the teaching of the Church on the sacrament of confirmation is contained, not in explicit doctrinal formulas, but in the Scriptures and in the liturgy of confirmation. Like all the sacraments, it must be seen in the perspective of the story of salvation and especially in the light of what divine revelation tells us of the action of the Holy Spirit. However theologians view the effects of the sacrament, all are agreed that confirmation is the sacrament that bestows the Holy Spirit in a special way. Just as we can say that baptism is the sacrament of the resurrection, so we can say that confirmation is the sacrament of the sending of the Spirit. As we associate baptism with Easter, so we associate confirmation with Pentecost. There is a deep-seated Catholic instinct about this which can arise only from the fact that these events are related to these sacraments and have always been associated with them in the minds of the faithful.

The examination of the texts of the baptismal liturgy gave us a more complete insight into the sacrament of baptism; we hope to show that an examination of the texts of the confirmation liturgy will give us the same deep understanding of confirmation. They include not only the rite itself, but also the texts of the liturgy of Pentecost and its octave in the missal and in the divine office.

Although the celebration of Pentecost can greatly illuminate the meaning and effects of confirmation, we must point out that there is no definite single passage in the Scriptures that clearly deals with its purpose, even though many give us an indication of what this purpose is. Only after looking at them all and making a synthesis of what they teach can we reach satisfactory conclusions.

The theology of confirmation is still developing. Theologians are abandoning too-narrow and artificial concepts for a more comprehensive and dynamic view of this sacrament's role in Christian life. Even then, not all are in accord as to the details. It can be said, however, that most of the development and enrichment of the understanding of confirmation has come from a return to the Scriptures and to the Fathers of the Church. This approach has given us a fresh outlook upon that sacrament which the Fathers called "The Seal of the Spirit."

The "matter" of the sacrament of confirmation is the anointing of the forehead with chrism; the "form" is, "I sign [or seal] you with the sign of the cross and I confirm you with the chrism of salvation in the name of the Father, and of the Son, and of the Holy Spirit. Amen."

This rite tells us much about the sacrament itself. Anointing with oil was the rite that consecrated kings and priests for their tasks in the Old Testament. In turn, these "anointed ones" pointed forward to a great Anointed One who was to come.

Jesus was and is, for Christian believers, the *Christós*, the Anointed One, of whom the prophets spoke. "The spirit of the Lord has rested upon me, whereby he has anointed me. . . ." (Is 61,1) Our Lord applied these words of the prophet Isaia to himself. He is the one anointed by God, consecrated and dedicated to the mission of accomplishing the work of redemption. As the preface of the Mass of the feast of Christ the King expresses it,

> You anointed your only begotten son the eternal High Priest and the King of the Universe with the oil of gladness, so that offering himself upon the altar of the Cross he might accomplish the mystery of redemption. (*Roman Missal*, feast of Christ the King)

The anointing of the Head is poured forth upon the members. They too are anointed (that is, consecrated) by the Spirit of God to become other Christs—other "anointed ones." In their own way they are priests, kings, and as we shall see, prophets. The oil with which we are anointed in confirmation is the chrism that makes us in the full sense Christians, other Christs.

In his lectures *On the Mysteries* St. Cyril of Jerusalem says:

> In the same way as Christ was truly crucified, truly buried, truly risen again, and as it has been granted to you in baptism to be crucified with him, buried with him, risen with him in a certain imitation, so it is with the chrisma. He was anointed with the spiritual oil of exultation, that is with the Holy Spirit, called the oil of exultation because he is the source of spiritual joy; and you have been anointed with perfumed oil and become partakers of Christ. (Lect. 21 *On the Mysteries* 3,2)

That is, just as baptism configures us to Christ dead and risen again, so confirmation configures us to Christ anointed by the Holy Spirit.

St. Cyril speaks of perfumed oil, and this is where the essence of the symbolism of the chrism lies. Chrism is no ordinary oil; it is a *perfumed* oil. The Eastern rites perfume the oil much more than we do in the West, but in both East and West it is an aromatic mixture. It signifies the good odor of Christ, the delightful fragrance of the life and personality of him whom we call the Abyss of all Virtues. In a double way, then, the chrism speaks to us of Christ—by its very name, which comes from the same word as his own, and by its fragrance, which calls to mind the fragrance of his perfections. The implication of its use is that the sacrament makes us share in the fragrance of Christ and in his virtues.

The "form" or words of this sacrament, "I sign you with the sign of the cross and I confirm you with the chrism of salvation" means "I *seal* you." (The Byzantine rite has "The seal of the gift of the Spirit.") We are marked with the sign of the cross as a seal is imprinted upon wax. The outward signing and sealing signify the inner grace that the sacrament bestows: the anointing of the Spirit. Since the sending of the Spirit not only conforms us to Christ in his passion, as all the sacraments do in one way or another, but also was made possible through the death of Christ upon the cross, the "seal" is made with the cross. Placing the cross upon the forehead has still another meaning: the confirmed is to profess his faith boldly before the world and is not to be ashamed of the cross of Christ.

Like baptism, confirmation has had several names in the course of its history, all of which give us some idea of the significance of the sacrament. The oldest name is the "imposition (or laying-on) of hands" which derives from *Acts* and was the original way of bestowing the sacrament. This was a traditional biblical gesture to signify the transmission of power or the giving of a blessing. Other ancient names are *"sphragis"* or *"signaculum"* (the seal), and *"consignatio"* (sealing), the name given confirmation in the Roman rite in early times.

Sphragís is biblical in origin. We meet it in Paul: "Now it is God who is warrant for you and for us in Christ who has anointed us, and stamped us with his seal and has given us the Spirit as a pledge in our hearts." (2 Cor 1,21f) In this passage, the three ideas are brought together: anointing, sealing, and the Holy Spirit.

Because of the anointing with chrism which formed the rite of confirmation by the fourth century, the sacrament itself was sometimes known as "the sacrament of chrism" or even simply as "the chrism." Only later in the West was the term *chrisma* (anointing) restricted to the *oil* used in the anointing.

In the East, the sacrament was called *"mýron,"* related to the word "myrrh" from the richly perfumed oil that was (and still is) used in the East for the anointing. Mary Magdalen anointed Jesus with ointment, "genuine nard of great value" (*mýron* in the Greek text of St. John's gospel) and the whole house was filled with the perfume. (Jn 12,3) From this the *mýron* came to symbolize the good odor of Christ, "the perfume of the gospel," which St. Paul tells us the Christian should spread everywhere he goes. (2 Cor 2,14f)

Other terms that have been used in the past for confirmation are *"consummatio"* and *"perfectio."* These terms appear to be synonymous, but it is likely that *"consummatio"* had in Christian Latin the special sense of consecration to God's service. *"Perfectio"* means that confirmation is the accomplishment or completion of baptism. This is the unanimous view of the Fathers about confirmation: it perfects baptism and completes the work that baptism has begun.

Finally there is the term "confirmation" itself, with the verb form "confirm" which has prevailed in the West and passed over into nearly all the European languages. Like the other terms it is ancient but does not appear as a technical name for confirmation until the fifth century. When "confirmation" was first used it was synonymous with perfection, completion. The confirmation of baptism was that contemplated, whereas we think of the confirmation of the one baptized. Like the term "perfection" the word confirmation originally stressed the *continuity* between the sacraments; our use of the term emphasizes their *separation* from one another. This is an important point to remember, because the change in the meaning of the term brought about a complete change in the understanding of the sacrament.

The modern use of the word dates from a homily on Pentecost given in the fifth century by an unknown preacher in Gaul, and later attributed to Pope Melchiades (311–14). It was included in the decretals of the popes and found its way in time into the *Sentences* of Peter Lombard, which was the standard textbook of theology for the middle ages up to the time of St. Thomas Aquinas. In this way a mediocre homily became one of the most frequently cited texts on confirmation. The author of this homily is responsible for the idea that confirmation is a "strengthening for battle" (*robur ad pugnam*) and that it makes a baptized person a soldier of Christ. He answers the question, "What does confirmation do for us that baptism hasn't already done?" by saying, "In baptism we are born again to life, after baptism we are strengthened for battle; in baptism we are washed, in confirmation we are strengthened."

We hope to show that this, although true enough, is a rather restrictive view. If anything, it emphasizes only one aspect of the strengthening and limits the word too much. The gift of fortitude is received in confirmation, or rather it is increased; that is true, but there is much more to confirmation. Also, the phrase "strength for battle" and the related "soldier of Christ" are, taken by themselves, a little too militaristic. Much warmer and richer is the biblical idea of being strengthened to bear witness to Christ or of receiving a share in the prophetic anointing of Christ.

THE ROLE OF THE HOLY SPIRIT
IN THE HISTORY OF SALVATION

Because the sacrament of confirmation bestows the Spirit in a special way, it can be really understood only in the context of the mission and work of the Spirit as it is shown us in revelation. What the sacrament of confirmation does is what the Spirit does. The role of the Spirit in the divine plan must be understood before we can adequately grasp what he does in confirmation.

The Holy Spirit is the Spirit of Jesus. He has no other purpose than to manifest Jesus and communicate him to us. The activity of the Spirit, in brief, is to bring about the divinization of mankind. He can rightly be called the chief agent of the divine plan of salvation, in that he is entrusted with the task of making new heavens and a new earth, of bringing about the new creation. He does this first by causing the incarnation itself, then by extending the incarnation in time and space. More specifically, he does it by raising Jesus from the dead and making him the firstfruits of a new humanity. Christ is himself the masterpiece of the Spirit, the pattern and the source of the new creation. It is in and through Christ that humanity is refashioned and reconstituted.

The Holy Spirit is seen at work in the Old Testament. The creation is attributed to the power that is the Spirit of God. Needless to say, there can be no question in the Old Testament of a distinct personal Spirit; the full revelation of any of the persons of the Trinity is given only in the New Testament. But by the light of that very New Testament revelation we are able to discover indications of his activity. The revelation of the Spirit, like all other revelation, is gradual. Such terms as "Spirit of Yahweh," "Spirit of

God," "Holy Spirit," "my Spirit" refer to the *"Ru'ah Yahweh,"* the breath or power of God.

We see this *Ru'ah,* or power, of Yahweh at work all through the Old Testament. It is life-giving power, a life-giving breath. The breath of God stirred over the waters and brought forth life from them. By the word of the Lord the heavens were made (Gen 1,2); by the breath of his mouth all their host. (Ps 32[33],6) Man, too, is created by having God breathe upon him: "The Lord God breathed into his nostrils the breath of life and he became a living being." (Gn 2,7) "For the spirit of God has made me, and the breath of the almighty keeps me alive." (Job 33,4)

Perhaps the clearest example of the life-giving property of the breath or spirit of Yahweh is seen in Ezechiel's vision of the dry bones. This is a most important text, for it is a parable of the resurrection of Israel and is one of the great prophecies of the messianic times. It is introduced by an earlier promise contained in Chapter 36, "I will cleanse you the people of Israel of all your iniquities and I will place a new spirit within you." The vision in the next chapter is a kind of advance demonstration of that promise. The prophet saw a field of dry bones that were joined together and covered with flesh and sinews and skin, but there was still no life in them because "there was no spirit in them."

> Thus says the Lord God: From the four winds come, O Spirit, and breathe into these slain that they may come to life. I prophesied as he told me and the spirit came into them; they became alive and stood upright, a vast army. Then he said to me: Son of Man, these bones are the whole house of Israel . . . O my people! I will put my spirit in you that you may live, and I will settle you upon your land; thus you shall know that I am the Lord. (Ez 37,9–11.14)

We see in this prophecy that the Spirit of God is to bring about a resurrection to new life for Israel. We notice too that the gift of the life-giving spirit is to be given to the *whole* people. The full meaning of this can be seen in the other prophecies about the outpouring of the Spirit.

The climax of the Old Testament revelation of the activity of the Spirit is found in the messianic prophecies. The age of the Messia was to be marked by a great outpouring of the Spirit. First of all, the Spirit of the Lord will rest upon the Messia and anoint him to fulfill his mission:

> There shall come forth a shoot
> from the stump of Jesse
> and a branch shall grow out of his roots.
> And the spirit of the Lord shall rest upon him
> the spirit of wisdom and understanding
> the spirit of counsel and might
> the spirit of knowledge and the fear of the Lord. (Is 11,1f)

53

This means that the Messia will be a man completely filled with the Spirit of the Lord, the breath of Yahweh. He will be possessed by this Holy Spirit, who will sanctify him and make him his instrument.

> The spirit of God is upon me
>   because the Lord has anointed me
> to bring good tidings to the afflicted.
>   He has sent me to bind up the broken-hearted
> to proclaim liberty to the captives
>   and the opening of the prison to those who are bound
> to proclaim the year of the Lord's favor. (Is 61,1f)

The mission of the Messia will be altogether under the guidance and direction of the *Ru'ah Yahweh,* the Spirit of Yahweh, and the Messia will in turn communicate the Spirit that possesses him to the whole house of Israel.

> And it shall come to pass on those days [the messianic times] that I shall pour forth my spirit on all flesh; your sons and your daughters shall prophesy, your old men shall dream dreams, and your young men shall see visions. Even upon the men servants and the maid servants in those days I will pour out my spirit. (Jl 3,1f)

The Spirit that rested upon the Messia will be poured out on all flesh; instead of resting intermittently upon the few, the Spirit will inspire all men to prophesy.

CONFIRMATION
IN THE NEW TESTAMENT

We can begin by saying that the New Testament is the era of the Holy Spirit. The gift of the Spirit is its characteristic gift. Christ's whole mission can be described simply as "to send the Holy Spirit." For this he died, rose again, and ascended into heaven: to pour out his own Spirit on mankind, to endow us with the greatest and best of his gifts. The role of the Spirit in the New Testament is to bring about in men the "new man who is created in justice and true holiness," that is, to bring forth other Christs.

The key passage for the evidence of the existence of confirmation in the New Testament is that of Acts 8,14–17:

> Now when the apostles at Jerusalem heard that Samaria had received the word of God [through the preaching of Philip] they sent to them Peter and John who came down and prayed for them that they might receive the Holy Spirit, for it had not yet fallen upon them but they had only been baptized in the name of the Lord Jesus. Then they laid hands on them and they received the Holy Spirit.

This is the only passage in the New Testament where the "laying-on of hands" which gives the Holy Spirit is clearly distinguished from baptism. If it stood altogether by itself, we would have to admit that the New Testament evidence for a distinct sacrament which we call confirmation is slight. But the passage *does not* stand altogether by itself even if it is the only one that clearly distinguishes the two sacraments. Later in the same book there is the incident wherein Paul encounters some people who had received the baptism of John. He asked them if they had received the Holy Spirit. Upon being told that they had not even heard of the Spirit, Paul instructs them in the meaning of Christian baptism. "On hearing this they were baptized in the name of the Lord Jesus. And when Paul had laid his hands upon them, the Holy Spirit came upon them and they spoke with tongues and prophesied." (Ac 19,5f) This passage almost exactly parallels the passage in Acts 8 and comes very close to making as clear a distinction. The Holy Spirit comes upon the disciples at the laying-on of hands, which takes place after baptism.

The teaching of the epistles alone is not clear, but in the light of the texts in Acts and of the later practice of the Church (both Tertullian and Cyprian allude to a laying-on of hands that gives the Holy Spirit), it is reasonable to believe that something more than baptism is meant in the following passages.

> The love of God has been spread abroad in our hearts through the Holy Ghost that was given to us. (Rom 5,5) We received . . . the spirit which is of God. (1 Cor 2,12) We were all made to drink of one spirit. (1 Cor 12,13) God sent forth the spirit of his son into our hearts crying Abba—Father. (Gal 4,6) He that anointed us is God, who also sealed us and gave us the earnest [the pledge] of the Spirit in our hearts. (2 Cor 1,21ff) In whom having also believed you were sealed with the Holy Spirit of promise. (Eph 1,13) Grieve not the Holy Spirit of God in whom you were sealed unto the day of redemption. (Eph 4,30) He saved us through the washing of regeneration and renewal of the Holy Spirit. (Tit 3,5) The anointing which you received of him abides in you. (1 Jn 2,27) For it is impossible to restore again to repentance those who have once been enlightened, who have tasted the heavenly gift, and have become partakers of the Holy Spirit and have tasted the goodness of the word of God and the powers of the age to come if they then commit apostasy. (Heb 6,4f)

One other passage in the epistles must be mentioned which in some ways is the most significant of all *if* it refers to confirmation. It is possible that it does, although most exegetes think it is a reference to ordination: "I remind you to rekindle the grace that is within you through the laying-on of my hands." (2 Tim 1,6)

In any case there is more than enough evidence in the other passages to create a strong probability, even if not an absolute certainty, of the existence of a special rite which conferred the Holy Spirit.

Especially significant are those passages which speak of the sealing and the anointing. They do not refer to a material anointing, of course, and one cannot support the anointing with oil from the pages of the New Testament. It is possible that such was the practice, since anointing with oil was the normal accompaniment of a bath in the Mediterranean world. There is no direct evidence to support its use; nevertheless the texts do indicate a reality which was expressed by the metaphor of sealing and anointing—the outpouring of the Spirit into the hearts of the faithful.

The seal was a symbol of the person, and the authority of the one that it belonged to; the image of the owner was sometimes graven upon it. This symbolism took on new meaning when Christ declared that he was marked with the seal of God his Father: ". . . For on him has God the Father set his seal." (Jn 6,27) In this case the seal is not only the power that God gives him to do his work, it is also the consecration that makes him the son of God, "whom the Father consecrated and sent into the world." (Jn 10,36) This is the consecration the Christian participates in when God marks him with his seal and gives him his Spirit. Thanks to this seal, men are able to be faithful to the divine will. It is a mark that shows they belong to God and is at the same time a power that keeps them faithful to his service.

HISTORY OF THE RITE

The first account of the ritual of confirmation is given in the Acts of the Apostles, when Peter and John came down to Samaria to bestow the sacrament on those Philip the deacon had baptized. The ritual was very simple: "They [the apostles] prayed for them that they might receive the Holy Spirit . . . then they laid hands on them and they received the Holy Spirit." (Ac 8,14–17) A prayer and the laying-on of hands, that is all. Nothing is said about anointing with oil. But there is a distinction between baptism, which Philip could give, and confirmation, which only the apostles could bestow.

In Africa nearly two centuries later, Tertullian describes the same ritual with a little more detail: "The hand is imposed in blessing, calling and inviting the Holy Spirit." (*On Baptism*, 8) The "blessing" may have been the same prayer that the apostles used. There is no mention of oil here, either.

A few years later, St. Cyprian, Bishop of Carthage, describes the rite of confirmation in one of his letters. "The newly-baptized person is presented to the head of the Church; he receives the Holy Spirit through our prayer and the imposition of our hand and is perfected by means of the Lord's sign [the sign of the cross]." (*Epistle* 73,9) This is a more detailed description than either of the others. We note incidentally that both Tertullian and Cyprian speak of one hand, though that does not necessarily mean that only one hand was used. Again there is no mention of oil.

The first complete description of the rite of confirmation comes to us in the *Apostolic Tradition* of Hippolytus, 22. Here we have the exact words of the prayer and also the first mention of chrism. After the rite of baptism is finished, the bishop places his hand on the candidate's head and says the prayer: "Lord God, who have made them worthy to obtain the remission of sins by means of regeneration of the Holy Spirit, send into them your grace that they may serve you according to your will, for yours is the glory, Father, Son, and Holy Spirit in the Holy Church, now and forever. Amen." After this first laying on of hands and prayer, the bishop then pours chrism into his hand and places it upon the person's head, saying, "I anoint you with holy oil in the Lord, the Father Almighty, Christ Jesus, and the Holy Spirit." Then he makes the sign of the cross on the forehead of the candidate and gives him the kiss of peace. We see that there are two impositions of the hand and that the anointing is on the head. The signing is distinct from the anointing.

Even though the anointing was included in the Roman rite of confirmation, from this time on the imposition of hands was still considered the "matter" of the sacrament. As late as the fifth century St. Leo I says that Christians "are to be confirmed only by means of an invocation of the Holy Spirit and the imposition of hands." (*Epistle* 159,7)

The shift of emphasis from the imposition of hands to the anointing with chrism was gradual. The anointing with oil seemed to be more symbolic of the inner anointing of the Holy Spirit than the laying-on of hands. It was natural that this anointing should tend to gain greater attention.

For some time both practices were maintained and given equal importance. But gradually the anointing with chrism came to prevail, at least in the minds of the theologians. Even St. Thomas Aquinas says that "the second sacrament is confirmation, whose matter is anointing with chrism" (*Opuscula,* IV, T27,179) and does not speak of the first imposition of hands. The *Decree for the Armenians* reflects the theological teaching of its time (1439) in stating that "the matter of confirmation is chrism blessed by the bishop and the form is '*Signo te signo crucis*'. . . ."

Nevertheless the liturgical books maintained the ancient practice of an individual imposition of hands before the anointing. But by the end of the thirteenth century, this had become the modern collective imposition which still occurs at the beginning of the rite when the bishop extends his hands toward those to be confirmed.

To supply the defect of an individual imposition of hands, Benedict XIV in the eighteenth century ordered that, in confirming, the bishop is to place his hand on the head of the one he is confirming while at the same time anointing him with the thumb.

In light of the historical evidence, we are compelled to admit that the Church seems to have changed the matter and form of this sacrament (the present form, for example, dates from only the thirteenth century; before that various forms were used).

On the other hand, when a minister of confirmation in the West anoints the forehead with his thumb, he at the same time places his hand upon the head within the ancient understanding of that gesture. We think of laying-on the hand as placing the hand on the top of the head, but that was only one way of "imposing hands" in the ancient world. From this we can conclude that it is by no means absolutely clear that the Western Church has changed the matter of the sacrament.

LATER DEVELOPMENTS

The growth in the number of baptisms, the multiplication of churches, and finally the fact that most of those baptized were infants, all made it difficult for the bishop himself to preside over the process of Christian initiation, as he had done in ancient times.

The two main sections of the Church each solved the problem in a different way. In the East priests were allowed to administer confirmation from the fourth century onward. But they had to use oil (*mýron*) consecrated by the bishop. In that way the East was able to keep up the ancient practice of administering baptism, confirmation, and the eucharist at the same service, even to infants. At the same time the rights of the bishop were safeguarded because technically the priest was acting as his deputy in admitting the baptized to confirmation.

Exactly the opposite solution was reached in the West. Instead of keeping the sacraments together, the West separated them; confirmation was deferred until the bishop could come to administer it. There was never any question of allowing priests to confirm until modern times.

As late as the ninth century the practice of confirming immediately after baptism was maintained in Rome. The pope himself confirmed the neophytes at the Lateran Basilica (during the Easter vigil), and other bishops confirmed in the parish churches of the city. In certain dioceses of Spain and Latin America bishops still confirm babies after baptism.

But in the rest of Europe, confirmation was progressively deferred until the fourth or seventh year after baptism. During the eighteenth and nineteenth centuries the age limit was still further extended; in many countries it was reserved until the candidates were twelve years old.

This excessive deferring of confirmation was entirely a matter of the triumph of custom over law, however. The Church has never officially approved the custom; the catechism of the Council of Trent calls for confirmation to be given when the use of reason has been reached. (*Catechismus Romanus*, II,3,15) The *Code of Canon Law* and the *Roman Ritual* say, "seven years." (*C.I.C.*, canon 788; *Rit. Rom*, tit.3, cap.3, n.11)

There seems to be no reason, therefore, why confirmation could not be given today before first communion. In that way the proper order of the sacraments of Christian initiation would be preserved. If that should not be possible for any reason, the only alternative, recommended by some modern liturgists, would be to give all priests who have the care of souls the faculty to confirm. The chrism would still have to be consecrated by the bishop of the diocese, and the priests would be acting as his representatives. The bishop would always remain the *ordinary* minister of confirmation and of course would himself confirm those whom he had baptized, either in his cathedral church or elsewhere.

THE MODERN RITUAL
OF CONFIRMATION

There are three parts to the modern rite of confirmation.

The General Laying-on of Hands

Standing with his hands joined before him, the bishop begins the rite with the brief prayer:

> May the Holy Spirit come upon you and may the power of the Most High preserve you from sins. Amen.

This prayer is relatively modern; we meet it for the first time in the twelfth century *Pontifical* of the Roman Curia. There follow the three versicles and responses which are the customary introductions to blessings. They too are modern, having been added by Bishop William Durand (d. 1296).

Then, extending his hands out over these to be confirmed, he says:

> Almighty, eternal God, who in your kindness have given to these your servants a new birth through water and the Holy Spirit, and granted them remission of all their sins, send forth from heaven upon them your sevenfold Spirit, the Paraclete,
> The spirit of wisdom and understanding. Amen.
> The spirit of counsel and fortitude. Amen.
> The spirit of knowledge and piety. Amen.
>
> Mercifully fill them with the spirit of your fear and seal them with the sign of the cross of Christ that they may obtain eternal life. Through our Lord. . . .

This prayer is called the *"epíklēsis"* because it calls down the Holy Spirit. Basically it is the same as the prayer of St. Hippolytus, quoted earlier, but it has been enlarged to include the enumeration of the gifts of the Holy Spirit. In its present form it dates from the seventh or eighth century. It is of great value for an understanding of the meaning of confirmation as the gift of the Spirit. The bishop's reference to God's servants having received a new birth of water and the Holy Spirit implies that these people have just been baptized, and so goes back to the time when confirmation immediately followed baptism.

The Spirit who will descend upon the believers is the Spirit who rested upon Jesus at his baptism, the Spirit who filled the human soul of Jesus and anointed him as the Messia. The enumeration of the gifts of the Spirit is taken from Isaia and describes the endowment of the Messia.

The seal is the *sphragís,* the mark of Christ. Confirmation is the seal of the Spirit, the anointing that sets a man apart and consecrates him. The seal is nothing less than the likeness of Christ crucified impressed upon the soul.

The Signing of the Candidates

After that the bishop makes the sign of the cross on the forehead of each person with his right thumb, which has been dipped in chrism, saying as he does so "I sign [seal] you with the sign of the cross, and I confirm you with the chrism of salvation, in the name of the Father and of the Son and of the Holy Spirit. Amen."

A variety of formulas was used in the past, from the first one quoted earlier, in the *Apostolic Tradition,* to the simpler, "The sign of the cross unto eternal life," and even to simply, "In the name of the Father, and of the Son, and of the Holy Spirit." The present formula is merely one that has survived out of all these.

"I sign you" here probably means "seal" and would seem to be more in keeping with the act of anointing, which also means to seal. The Byzantine rite uses the formula, "The seal of the gift of the Holy Spirit," and anoints not only the head but the various senses.

After he has anointed the one confirmed, the bishop gives him or her a light slap on the cheek, saying as he does so, "Peace be with you." As the words indicate, we are dealing here with a rite that has been changed from its original form. Obviously, it was at first nothing more than the kiss of peace, like that in the ordination rite. The *"alapa,"* as the blow is called, was introduced into the rite by Bishop Durand. It probably derives from a Frankish custom of striking someone lightly on the cheek to make him remember a contract that he had made.

The Concluding Rite

After all have been confirmed, the choir sings the antiphon, "Strengthen and fortify what you have done in us, from the height of your temple on high which is in the heavenly Jerusalem." This antiphon, obviously selected for its opening word as well as for the ideas it contains, was added by Durand. It is taken from Psalm 67[68], one of the great Pentecost psalms in the Roman liturgy. It is a prayer that God will make the grace of confirmation effective in us and that the Spirit who has come down from heaven upon us will complete the work he has begun in us.

The brief dialogue customary before prayers in the Roman liturgy leads up to the final prayer, which goes back to the tenth century. It is addressed to Christ:

> Lord God, you gave the Holy Spirit to your disciples and have willed that by them and their successors he should be handed on to the rest of the faithful. Look graciously upon our humble ministry and grant that the Holy Spirit may descend upon those whom we have sealed upon the forehead with the anointing of holy chrism and the sign of your holy cross. May he dwell there to make them the temple of your glory.

Just as the Holy Spirit dwelt in the soul of Jesus and made it holy, and as he came down upon the apostles to make them prophets and witnesses, so now he comes to each Christian to continue in him the work of the incarnation and the redemption. The wonder of Pentecost is renewed, without the striking outward manifestations that marked that event but no less really and completely.

A final blessing concludes the whole rite:

> See how each one who fears the Lord is blessed! May the Lord bless you from the heavenly Zion, and may you obtain all the good things of Jerusalem all the days of your life and eternal life at the end. Amen.

The blessings of the new covenant—sonship, joy, life, intimacy with God—are "the good things of Jerusalem" which God bestows through the working of the Holy Spirit in us. We enjoy them in this life, but they are ordered and directed toward the final object of the divine plan: eternal life in the Jerusalem that is above. They secure that life for us in advance and bring us safely to the eternal possession of it.

When confirmation began to be separated from baptism, around the year 1000, the church became the usual place for the administration of the sacrament (earlier it had been given in a room in the baptistery called the *consignatorium*). Oddly enough, bishops in the Middle Ages often used to confirm in the fields or by the roadside, wherever they found anyone (usually babies) who had not been confirmed.

THE EFECTS OF CONFIRMATION

The fact that the rite of Christian initiation was a single process for so many centuries makes it almost impossible to assign specific effects to each of the sacraments of baptism and confirmation. We can determine such effects only from the texts themselves, relying upon later practice to give us a clue. The New Testament writers spoke of the effect of the redemption as a whole, without distinguishing too much (or perhaps enough) the role of each of these rites in the scheme of things.

The key to the whole problem seems to be in remembering that, according to Christian tradition going back to the third century, confirmation completes and perfects baptism. There is no need, therefore, of trying to discover something altogether different given in confirmation from what is given in baptism. Some theologians, such as the late Gregory Dix, thought that the remission of sins was all that was given in baptism whereas the Spirit was given only in confirmation. But there is absolutely no warrant for thus deforming the sacrament of baptism. As we have seen, baptism is the sacrament of new birth. New birth is so often connected with the bath of water that one cannot hold otherwise. But new birth is impossible without the action of the Spirit—that Spirit who raised Jesus from the dead, who also quickens our mortal bodies to life.

Therefore we may say that confirmation does not add anything new to baptism, nor give us anything we do not already have. But it completes, brings to full development, what is already there. That is why we must say that so many of the Scripture texts that refer to baptism also refer to confirmation. On the other hand, there are Scripture texts which refer verbally to baptism, but the fullness of what is connoted there is attained only through confirmation. The classic example, of course, is the Pentecost-event itself, because Pentecost was at once the baptism and the confirmation of the infant Church.

In treating of the relationship of baptism to confirmation, we must not forget that there is no opposition between the two, as though either one were a rival of the other. Rather there is continuity between them, and the development of the same process of sanctification. Baptism is a sacrament in its own right; it remits sin and gives grace. It could not do these things unless it gave the Holy Spirit. Precisely because baptism engenders in us life *in* the Spirit and the life *of* the Spirit, it awaits that completion and fullness which is necessary to make the baptized believer a perfect Christian. We use the word "perfect" not in the moral sense but in the ontological sense, descriptive, as it were, of the difference between a child and a grown man. The child is a human being, a man in the physical sense, but he is not a perfect man until he grows up. A comparison such as this is imperfect and incomplete, but it will serve to convey what is meant by calling confirmation the perfection and completion of baptism. By this sacrament the believer's being as a Christian is completed. He is clothed with the fullness of the Spirit after the likeness of Christ. In fact, the clue to the relationship of the two sacraments lies here. They both have for their aim to conform the believer to Christ, to reproduce Christ in him.

The Life of Christ Reproduced in the Christian

In the life of Christ there were two "anointings" by the Spirit. The first was at the moment of the incarnation; that one established him as the Son of God: "The Holy Spirit will come upon you and the power of the Most High will overshadow you, therefore, the child to be born of you will be called holy, the son of God." (Lk 1,35) By this anointing which is the hypostatic union, Jesus was constituted king and priest at the same time. It was his *royal* and *priestly* consecration.

The other anointing took place when he was baptized in the Jordan. At that moment he accepted his mission as "suffering servant" and messia-redeemer. He was anointed then as the great agent of the divine plan of salvation. This was his *prophetical* anointing.

These two separate, yet related, anointings must be reproduced in the life of the Christian. The first anointing of the Spirit takes place at baptism, making him the adopted son of God. The second takes place at confirmation when the Spirit descends upon him again to make him a prophet, to equip him with the gifts he needs to enable him to live fully the life of an adopted son, and to fulfill his mission in the Church. In confirmation he is empowered to function properly as a member of the priestly people, that is, to offer God spiritual and true worship in the true temple which is the body of Christ, the Church.

Jesus was anointed with the Spirit at the time of his baptism, but it was at Pentecost that the apostles were anointed by the Spirit. The Spirit we receive in confirmation is the Spirit of Pentecost. That confirmation is the individual Christian's Pentecost is shown by the prayer at the end of the rite of confirmation:

> God, who gave the Holy Spirit to your apostles and have willed that through them and their successors he be given to the rest of the faithful, look with favor on our humble service and grant that the Holy Spirit descending into the heart of this man/woman whose forehead we have anointed with holy chrism and signed with the sign of the holy cross may, by dwelling there, make it a temple of his glory.

The Fathers and Doctors of the Church follow the same line of argument to show the effects of confirmation: what happened on Pentecost happens now to the individual Christian. The Church, in the Council of Florence (1439), declared that,

> The effect of this sacrament consists in this, that the Holy Spirit is given for the strengthening of the Christian, just as he was given to the apostles on the day of Pentecost, the purpose being that the Christian may boldly profess the name of Christ.

The Spirit Active in the Church Through Confirmation

Preachers are fond of pointing out that the descent of the Holy Spirit transformed the little band of timid apostles into courageous witnesses for Christ. Before this they were afraid, now they were afraid no longer; threats and punishments could not silence them from boldly professing Christ and proclaiming his gospel.

The same Spirit is given to us and he produces the same effects. He moves us now, in the twentieth century, to proclaim the gospel courageously according to our place in the Church. This does not mean that we are to be violent or forward or insolent. It does mean professing our faith whatever the cost. One very obvious way of professing the faith is to take part in public worship. In fact, as we have seen, to prophesy is to praise God and to proclaim what he has done. The worship of God is one of the aspects of the prophetic ministry of the Church and so of the individual member of the Church.

To proclaim the gospel does not mean preaching in the ordinary sense of the word. For most of us our professing and proclaiming is done by the kind of life we lead. Americans are told that when they travel in foreign countries they should not forget that they represent their country in these foreign lands in an unofficial way. People will judge the United States by the way Americans act away from home. Confirmation makes us representatives of the Church and witnesses to Christ before the whole world. Our manner of living and acting should be worthy of this vocation.

The prayer for the consecration of the chrism asks that God will send the power of the Spirit into this chrism "with which you have anointed priests, kings, prophets and martyrs." The chrism itself and the sacrament of chrism are thus shown to prepare men for martyrdom. We might say that a martyr is a witness with a capital "W," for he or she is one who has witnessed even unto death. In fact, that is why "martyr" has acquired its modern technical sense, for "martyr" originally meant simply a witness.

Confirmation is not associated with martyrdom needlessly, for it is the constant teaching of the Church that this sacrament gives us the strength to profess our faith even unto death, if need be. It takes courage and fortitude to die for our beliefs, but if that should be necessary confirmation gives us the grace to do it.

Spiritual Maturity: The Sevenfold Gift of the Spirit

Confirmation fills us with the sevenfold Spirit and brings the Christ-life to full maturity and development in us. In the natural order we attain full maturity only after long years, but in the order of grace we attain the full development of the Christ-life in a few moments by the power of the Spirit of God. Regardless of our age, confirmation grants us the full complement of our endowment of divine sonship. We must develop it, but nevertheless we have it. It is not a question of physiological or psychological maturity, nor even of ascetical maturity. It is, so to speak, ontological maturity, a maturity of Christian being.

The first effect of this sacrament, therefore, is to bestow on us the fullness of the Spirit and so to transform the baptized person into a "perfect Christian." According to St. Thomas, in his treatise on confirmation, this sacrament makes us attain to full spiritual stature, "the perfect age, as it were, of the supernatural life." (S.Th., 3,72,1 c) In saying this St. Thomas is only echoing the whole tradition of the Church going back to the Fathers, who always regarded this sacrament as the seal of the Spirit which completes baptism. In confirmation the Spirit does in us what he did in Christ. The whole mystery of Christ (which includes the Church) is the masterpiece of the Spirit.

It was his own Spirit that Jesus poured forth abundantly on Pentecost, with the mission of continuing among men the mystery of the incarnation. This is the Spirit poured out on us in confirmation. Its mission in us is the same: to bring us to the full measure of the age of Christ.

Just as Jesus needed the presence and the action of the Spirit to realize to the full God the Father's design in him, we need the same Spirit to realize the divine plan in us. The divine plan is that we should be conformed to Christ, be made in his likeness.

The seven gifts of the Spirit effect a smoother functioning of the life of Christ in us. They render us more prompt to respond to the urgings of the Spirit, the demands that the Christ-life makes upon us. Insofar as we can say such a thing, they make it easier for us to live the supernatural life; they make it, as it were, natural. Under the impulse of the gifts we find it relatively easy to withstand temptation, to pray, to worship, to follow the right course of action. It is true that this presupposes cooperation and the right dispositions on our part, but the gifts are there for the using. Again the difference between the saints and most of us is that they make use of the gifts to the full while so many of us let them remain idle.

Further Configuration to Christ the Priest

If confirmation is the completion of baptism (as all the ancient patristic and liturgical texts indicate) we can grasp the nature of this completion only in the light of baptism. We must ask what baptism itself does, for the completion of this baptism must be along the same lines. As we have seen, baptism has two main effects: it confers on us divine (adopted) sonship, and it consecrates us to God's service and worship (by the character). In order to be a true completion, then, confirmation must in some way bring these effects to perfection. There can be no other effect altogether different from these, but only a maturing, ripening, and deepening of our consecration to God and of our sonship of the heavenly Father.

65

The difference between baptism and confirmation is the difference between giving life and enabling that life to reach its full potential. Confirmation gives us the power to be what we already are by baptism. By baptism we are configured to Christ the priest; we became the members of a priestly people, deputed to the worship of God. This was the effect of the character, the seal bearing the likeness of Christ the priest that was stamped on our soul in baptism. Confirmation, by configuring us to Christ the prophet, completes the likeness to Christ the priest, because these two functions are intimately related.

Theologians dispute about whether a new character is conferred in confirmation which is different from the character of baptism, but this does not seem likely. Rather, it seems to be the same character, only deepened and intensified. For the character itself is by definition a power that makes us share in Christ's priesthood. There cannot be a character that is not in some way related to the priesthood of Christ. All that is possible is a further sharing in that priesthood; a greater aptitude to perform priestly acts.

Others make a distinction in this regard, saying that baptism gives us a passive deputation to worship whereas confirmation gives us an active deputation enabling us to engage in social worship. But this is surely inconsistent with the true notion of worship. The worship of the Church is social *by nature*. There is nothing passive about any of it. Baptism by its nature gives us a right to engage actively in the worship of the Church; confirmation cannot give us what we already have by baptism. Again it can only be a question of giving us a fuller deputation, or if you like, a more perfect deputation to that worship. Baptism has already made us members of the priestly community but confirmation strengthens and completes that membership.

This, it seems, is the real reason why one should be confirmed before being allowed to make his first communion. To receive communion at all is to profess one's faith before an unbelieving world. Confirmation enables us to do that. Furthermore, to receive communion is not only to obtain the nourishment necessary for our souls; it is an act of worship, a priestly act. To engage in an act of worship we should have the full equipment required to perform that act. This is why we should receive confirmation before first communion.

The whole source of our difficulty in fitting confirmation into the scheme of things arises from our having fallen into the practice of deferring it too long after baptism. If it were conferred either immediately after, or after only a reasonable interval as the *Code of Canon Law* requires, much of the speculation about confirmation would be seen to be unnecessary, because such speculation has arisen mainly from an attempt to meet a situation never contemplated by the early Church.

The requirement of modern Church law that children in danger of death be confirmed, by the parish priest if no bishop is available, should point the way to an ideal solution of the whole problem. St. Thomas said that babies in danger of death should be confirmed so as not to be deprived of the perfection of glory in heaven. Why, then, should infants *not* in danger of death be deprived of the perfection of grace on earth which brings them to the perfection of glory in heaven? If we baptize infants, why cannot we confirm them too? Even infants can be adults in grace. These considerations lead us to say that even if confirmation is not absolutely necessary for salvation, one cannot attain to the perfection of Christian life without it.

The ordinary minister of confirmation is the bishop of the diocese, because he is the head of the community. It is entirely fitting that the head of the community should complete the process of Christian initiation, just as he is properly the administrator of all sacraments and sacramentals to his flock.

The *Constitution on the Sacred Liturgy* (Article 72) suggests that confirmation be given at Mass immediately after the gospel. This illustrates very well the relationship between confirmation and the eucharist. Confirmation, like baptism, leads us to the altar of sacrifice and the table of the Lord.

The liturgy is the summit and the source of all the
activity of the Church. At its center is the sacrificial
meal which is the memorial of Christ's passion, resurrection, and ascension (Courtesy The Dumbarton Oaks
Collections).

CHAPTER THREE

THE
HOLY EUCHARIST

The third sacrament of Christian initiation is the eucharist, which is the consummation of the whole process. Baptism and confirmation exist for the eucharist. They prepare for it and lead up to it. Christian initiation is really initiation into the eucharistic mystery. The object and the goal of the process of Christian initiation is to bring us to live the eucharistic life. Baptism and confirmation depute us to worship, but that worship reaches its high point in the eucharistic sacrifice. Only through the eucharist are we able to offer God those "spiritual sacrifices" acceptable to him, that "spiritual service" which our baptism demands of us. Baptism and confirmation demand the eucharist as their completion because their function is to incorporate us more perfectly into Christ. But in the eucharist we come into direct contact with the glorious body of Christ. He abides in us and we in him. The eucharist therefore accomplishes complete incorporation into Christ.

The bond of union between these three sacraments is the paschal mystery, the central mystery of the Christian life. Baptism draws its power and its effectiveness from the paschal mystery, as we have seen. But the eucharist *is* the paschal mystery, made present in signs and symbols. "Making memorial of the blessed passion, the resurrection from the grave, and the ascension into glory, we your servants and also your holy people offer you a victim that is pure, a victim that is holy, a victim that is undefiled—the holy bread of eternal life and the cup of everlasting salvation." These words of the canon of the Mass tell what the Church is doing when she offers sacrifice to God. We (the whole Church) are doing this, that is, we are making a re-presentation of the whole mystery of redemption.

Baptism gives us life but the eucharist maintains us in life. The eucharist not only gathers the members of the Church together to offer sacrifice to God but it joins the members one to another in joining them to Christ. For these reasons the eucharist has always been considered by the Fathers and the liturgy as the symbol and sign of the unity of the mystical body; it is the sign of the Church as well as the sign of the sacrifice of Christ. Baptism and confirmation set us on the road that leads to the promised land—the messianic banquet of heaven—whereas the eucharist is the pledge and the anticipation of heaven. This is what we learn from singing the "Holy, Holy, Holy" at Mass: while still on earth we are engaged in what will be our eternal concern in heaven. Through the eucharistic sacrifice we join with angels and archangels to sing the never-ending hymn of God's glory. This is not only a pledge that what we do now we will be doing for eternity; it is an anticipation of it. We are *already* doing it.

The eucharistic meal is an anticipation of the messianic banquet in heaven; the guarantee that we will one day sit down with Abraham and Isaac and Jacob in the kingdom of heaven. More than food to sustain us on the journey, the eucharist is already journey's end. What we possess now under signs and figures we will one day possess forever, unveiled. This is the teaching of the postcommunion prayer of the feast of Corpus Christi:

> Grant, Lord, that we may come to that eternal enjoyment [that is, possession] of your godhead which the receiving of your body and blood here in time prefigures.

These words sum up the constant teaching of the Church that the eucharist is, as St. Ignatius of Antioch said in the second century, the "medicine of immortality, the antidote against eternal death."

The relationship between baptism and the eucharist is brought out in striking fashion by the Fathers in their baptismal catecheses. St. Ambrose, for example, shows the neophyte as hastening toward the heavenly banquet as if to say, "This is what I came for, this is the goal of my journey":

> Having laid aside the old clothing of the ancient error, his youth renewed like the eagle's he hastens toward the heavenly banquet. He arrives and seeing the holy altar prepared cries out "You have prepared a table for me." (*On the Mysteries,* 43)

The relationship between the two sacraments is more completely developed by the Eastern writer Theodore of Mopsuestia who like all the bishops of his time explains the sacred mysteries in the language of the Scriptures:

> In the same way as we receive the birth of baptism by means of the death of Christ, so also with our food. We receive it sacramentally by means of his death . . . to take the oblation and participate in the mysteries is to commemorate the death of our Lord which gains resurrection and the hope of immortality for us. For it is fitting that we, who have received a sacramental birth through the death of Christ, should receive the nourishment of the sacrament of immortality through the same death. We must be nourished from the same source from which we are born. (*Homily 15, 6*)

Both baptism and the eucharist are paschal sacraments, participation in Christ the risen Lord, who has passed through death. But the participation in the pasch achieved in the eucharist is greater than that achieved in baptism, for the mystery of the dying and rising is more perfectly present in the eucharist.

The process of Christian initiation is never really completed in this life. It needs to be renewed constantly. Through the eucharist each Christian is enabled to rediscover the meaning of baptism, confirmation, and the eucharist itself. The eucharist enables him to renew his Christian initiation, to perfect and complete it until his assimilation to Christ crucified and risen is perfected.

This is what we mean when we say that the eucharist is a sacrament of Christian initiation: it continues the process until death and makes us "become what we already are."

THE REVELATION OF THE DOCTRINE
OF THE EUCHARIST

The doctrine of the eucharist is basic to the whole New Testament; we can say that it is presupposed in almost every line and syllable. Without it, understood in its full Catholic sense, there would be no New Testament to speak of. For only through the eucharist is the new covenant possible.

Only because men eat the flesh of the Son of Man and drink his blood do they have the life of Emmanuel, "God-with-us," in them. The prophecies about the messianic reign do not and cannot reach their fulfillment except through the working of this sacrament, which continues the redemptive incarnation in our midst. Even in the days of his mortal flesh Christ was not so close to his Church, so present to her, as he is now through this sacrament.

It is hardly, therefore, a question of presenting the revelation of the doctrine in the old-fashioned apologetic manner, but rather of approaching it from the standpoint of salvation-history. The entire system of sacraments, once accepted, demands the existence of a sacrament that would unite us to the sacred humanity as closely as food is united to the body. Once that is understood, the next question is where and under what circumstances such a sacrament was revealed.

The answer can hardly be in the narrative of the institution alone, for the fact that Jesus gave little explanation of what he was doing indicates that there was some kind of previous preparation for this revelation. The accounts of the institution are valuable because they show that the tradition of the Church had already formed and crystallized by the time the gospels were written. Nevertheless, they presuppose an earlier instruction or many instructions in the meaning of what was done. We find this earlier instruction testified to in the sixth chapter of the gospel according to John.

St. John is the only evangelist who does not record the institution of the eucharist directly. He does hint at it in his account of the last supper and particularly in the introduction to the washing of the feet. On the other hand, he is the only evangelist who records the promise of the institution. This comes in the discourse after the multiplication of the loaves (which miracle the other three evangelists also record).

It is a long and quite complex discourse, falling into two parts. The first part revolves about the theme of the bread of life. Here Jesus presents himself as the bread of God which comes down from heaven and gives life to the world. "Jesus said to them I am the bread of life, he who comes to me will not hunger and he who believes in me shall never thirst. . . . I am the bread of life. Your fathers ate the manna in the wilderness, and they died. This is the bread that comes down from heaven that a man may eat of it and not die." (Jn 6,35.48ff) So far, the eucharistic meaning is not clear and the assimilation of which he speaks is chiefly by faith.

But the second part leaves little doubt as to Jesus' meaning: "I am the living bread that comes down from heaven; if any one eats this bread, he will live forever and the bread which I shall give is my flesh for the life of the world." (Jn 6,51) We must still apprehend Jesus by faith but the manner in which we are to come in contact with him is more clearly shown. He is the bread from heaven; in eating the bread he gives us we feed upon him.

72   Truly, truly I say to you, unless you eat of the flesh of the Son of
man and drink his blood you have no life in you; he who eats my

flesh and drinks my blood has eternal life and I will raise him up at the last day. For my flesh is meat indeed and my blood is drink indeed. He who eats my flesh and drinks my blood has eternal life and I will raise him up at the last day. He who eats my flesh and drinks my blood abides in me and I in him. . . . *This* is the bread that came down from heaven, not such as our fathers ate and died; he who eats this bread will live forever. (Jn 6,53–58)

In the first part of the discourse Jesus emphasized "coming to him" and believing in him; in the second part the emphasis is on eating—eating his flesh, eating him. He now clearly identifies the "bread of life" with his flesh and blood. It is also clear from the context that his hearers understood these words in the realistic sense: "How can this man give us his flesh to eat?" Apparently they understood that he was not speaking of "eating his flesh" in any cannibalistic sense. They knew that by "eating my flesh" he meant: assimilating me, being intimately united to me. Their difficulty lay in seeing how he would achieve this.

Jesus is therefore speaking of real eating. The mention of bread along with the miracle of the multiplication of the loaves suggested how this would be done. We feed upon what to all appearances is bread and by doing this we are feeding upon him.

The eucharist is therefore a means God has chosen of communicating the divine life to men. It is a perfect means because we cannot come any closer to the source of that divine life which is the sacred humanity of Christ. This divine life comes from the Father, dwells in Christ, and comes to us by the redeeming death of Christ. The bread of life is the body that was broken for us. "The bread I will give is my flesh [offered] for the life of the world." Hence the eucharist is above all the memorial of the passion. It re-presents Christ's redeeming death for us and makes it possible for us to unite ourselves to it by uniting ourselves to him who underwent it on our behalf.

St. John also shows us the effect of this sacred sacrificial banquet. It is union with Christ. (Notice we say union with *Christ,* not union with *God,* for our union with God can only be by union with Christ. We come to God *only* through the sacred humanity; this cannot be repeated often enough.) "He who eats my flesh and drinks my blood abides in me and I in him." Union with Christ gives life: "As the living Father has sent me and as I live because of the Father, so he who eats me shall also live because of me." (Jn 6,57) The life we live is the divine life, a share in the life of the Trinity. It is eternal life because "he who eats my flesh and drinks my blood has eternal life and I shall raise him up on the last day." (Jn 6,54)

All the chief effects of the eucharist are here: union with Christ (and so with one another, for the life we live is a *shared* life), union with the cross and the resurrection, and finally the pledge of future glory.

We can readily see from even this superficial look at the eucharistic discourse in St. John that the apostles could not have been much taken by surprise when, seated at the last supper, Christ said, "Take and eat, this is my body. Take and drink, this is the blood which shall be shed for you and for many unto the remission of sins."

The teaching given by John is reinforced by the teaching of St. Paul in such passages as, "as often as you eat this bread and drink the cup you proclaim the death of the Lord until he comes." (1 Cor 11,26) That this is not merely a ritual proclaiming is clear from the rest of the sentence about eating this bread and drinking the blood of the Lord unworthily. Such a one is guilty of sacrilege. This could not be the case if it were ordinary bread and wine.

Another explicit Pauline passage is: "The cup of blessing that we bless, is it not a sharing of the blood of Christ? And the bread that we break, is it not the partaking of the body of the Lord?" Then he adds: "Because the bread is one we though many are one because we partake of this one bread." (1 Cor 10,16f)

Furthermore, by saying that the eucharist proclaims the death of the Lord until he comes, Paul emphasizes the eschatological character of the eucharist; it is the "great sign" of the coming marriage-feast of the Lamb. It is the anticipation of the messianic banquet which at the same time prepares us to take part in it.

THE EUCHARIST—SACRIFICE AND SACRAMENT

At the Last Supper, on the night when he was betrayed, our Savior instituted the eucharistic sacrifice of his body and blood. He did this in order to perpetuate the sacrifice of the Cross throughout the centuries until he should come again, and so to entrust to his beloved spouse, the Church, a memorial of his death and resurrection: a sacrament of love, a sign of unity, a bond of charity, a paschal banquet in which Christ is eaten, the mind is filled with grace, and a pledge of future glory is given to us. (*Constitution on the Sacred Liturgy*, Article 47)

For the liturgy, "through which the work of our redemption is accomplished," most of all in the divine sacrifice of the eucharist, is the outstanding means whereby the faithful may express in their lives, and manifest to others, the mystery of Christ and the true nature of the Church. (Article 2)

In like manner, as often as they eat the supper of the Lord, they proclaim the death of the Lord until he comes. (Article 6)

Nevertheless the liturgy is the summit toward which the activity of the Church is directed; at the same time it is the fount from which all her power flows. For the aim and object of apostolic works is that all who are made sons of God by faith and baptism should come together to praise God in the midst of his Church, to take part in the sacrifice, and to eat the Lord's supper. (Article 10)

These quotations from the latest teaching of the Church on the liturgy may serve as a guide to the study of the sacrament of the eucharist. We should approach it as the living action of the living Church, as in fact the chief activity of the body of Christ. It is the supper of the Lord, the sacrificial meal of the mystical body, the memorial of Christ's death and resurrection, the source of grace and glory, the heart and center of the Church's life.

The eucharist is primarily not an abstract mystery of theology, still less of philosophy, but the mystery of salvation. It is above all a divine reality that can be rightly approached only with faith and love. Instead of dissecting and analyzing the truth it contains, we must contemplate the reality which the eucharistic sign embodies. This means that of all the sacraments, we must treat the eucharistic mystery as an action, the action of Christ and his Church.

Like the other sacraments, this sacrament must be studied for what it is, and according to its nature. Since it is a sacred sign we must study the *whole* sign in all its biblical and liturgical dimensions. Only in this way can we discover the full doctrine of the eucharist. For the doctrine is mediated to us through the entire complex of rites, prayers, chants, and readings that present the mystery to us in its fullness. This means in practice that the eucharistic mystery must be seen in the context of the *whole* Mass, which, after all, constitutes the complete sign of the mystery. If we confine our attention only to the words of consecration, to the essential matter and form, we will not get a complete view of the riches of eucharistic doctrine. To study the doctrine of the eucharist without ever adverting to the words of the great eucharistic prayer is to risk never understanding what the eucharist is.

In the past we have failed to study the eucharist as a whole and still less as something that people *do*. The time-honored approach still found in some theological manuals is to consider first the real presence, then the eucharist as sacrifice, and finally the sacrament as received. This is unfortunate in many ways, chiefly because it destroys the unity of the subject and considers each of these sections more or less in isolation from the others. Any such treatment prevents people from getting a view of the mystery as a whole.

If this method was unfortunate when used in theology books, it was nothing short of disastrous when transferred to religion manuals and catechisms for the use of the laity. It meant that in the minds of many people the sacrifice was separated from communion. Many even today do not see that communion is part of the Mass, that communion is a sharing in the sacrifice. We do share in the offering of the sacrifice by being present at Mass with the right dispositions; however, communion is the highest form of participation in the sacrifice, the most personal and intense form, we might say. Failure to appreciate this leads to failure to appreciate the true role of communion, which is to unite us with Christ in his sacrifice. Consequently many people regard communion as a consolation rather than as a means of strengthening us to take up our cross daily and follow Christ.

Another effect of this method of approaching the eucharist is that it tends to separate devotion to the real presence from devotion to the eucharistic sacrifice. So much is this true that many think of devotion to the eucharist as devotion to our Lord present in the tabernacle. They completely divorce that devotion from the Mass, which, after all, *provides* the real presence. The very way we use the word "eucharist" shows that we think of the whole mystery in a very different way than did the early Church, the Fathers, and the great later theologians such as St. Thomas. To the early Church the eucharist was the sacrificial meal. It was regarded then exactly as the *Constitution on the Liturgy* now regards it: as the supper of the Lord, the supper that is a sacrifice precisely because our Lord is present as priest and victim. Devotion to the holy eucharist is first of all devotion to the Mass.

One reason, if not the chief reason, why so much stress has been laid upon the real presence is that so many of the reformers denied it. Catholic apologists became obliged to defend the doctrine, and the effect of defending any doctrine is in the long run to present a one-sided picture of that doctrine. The way to defend the real presence of our Lord in the eucharist is to see the eucharist itself in the entire perspective of the story of salvation. If the mystery of our redemption is accomplished as often as this sacrifice is celebrated, our Lord *must* be present. If the sacraments are actions of Christ which continue his redeeming work, then he *must* be present in all of them, but especially in this one, the living memorial of his redeeming work.

Another defect in the method that held sway for so long in the teaching of the doctrine of the eucharist was that it separated the mystery from the rites that express it. With such a method it was possible to study the eucharist without ever opening the missal or looking at any of the prayer formulas, even the great eucharistic prayer itself. The words of consecration were indeed studied but almost always from a purely apologetical point of view. The effect of this is again to make the eucharist into an abstract truth to be defended rather than a mystery to be lived.

The sacred rites included in the entire Mass-action help us live this mystery. They show us with what faith and devotion we are to approach it and take part in it. The words of consecration taken by themselves cannot give us a complete view of the sacred mystery we are celebrating; they occur in the setting of a much longer prayer which unfolds, expands, and develops their meaning.

In turn that prayer (the great prayer, or canon) is infused with biblical language which evokes the whole sweep of the story of God's dealing with men. Its background and setting is altogether biblical. Furthermore, it does not stand by itself but comes after a fairly long introductory service of prayers and readings from the Scriptures. The liturgy of the word is the necessary introduction to the liturgy of the sacrifice.

The Church does not present the eucharistic mystery to us abruptly but surrounds it with a complex of rites and prayers which themselves become eucharistic by association. The whole Mass is eucharistic. The note of praise and worship that sounds loudest at the heart of the eucharistic action is present from the very beginning.

Whatever reasons there may have been in the past for a piecemeal approach to the eucharistic mystery, we know that we must return to the *traditional* approach which obtained in the Church until the Council of Trent and even later.

Especially in the light of the *Constitution on the Sacred Liturgy* we have no choice but to deal with the mystery of the eucharist from the biblical and pastoral viewpoint. This means we shall have to consider it as the celebration of the paschal mystery: as the supper of the Lord and the sacrifice of the Church. We must take into account all that has been written, said, and done in the past fifty years, our ultimate object being to understand the eucharist in the context of the Scriptures and the Church as the *summit* of the liturgy.

Seeing the eucharist in the context of the Church means that the point of departure is the Mass as it should be celebrated in parish churches on Sundays and feast days. We must view it as a corporate action in which all have their part to play. "Liturgical functions are not private functions, but are celebrations of the Church, which is the 'sacrament of unity,' namely, the holy people united and ordered under their bishops." (*Constitution on the Sacred Liturgy*, Article 26) We cannot consider the Mass in the abstract, isolated from the community. For although "every Mass [including one celebrated alone] has of itself a public and social character," this is not what our Lord had in mind when he instituted the eucharist. He intended that we should do what he did: "gather together to celebrate the Lord's supper."

> Therefore liturgical services pertain to the whole body of the Church—*they manifest it* and *have effects upon it,* but they concern the individual members of the Church in different ways according to their differing rank, office and actual participation. (*CSL,* Art. 26)

That is why the next number in the Constitution says that,

> It is to be stressed that whenever rites, according to their specific nature, make provision for communal celebration involving the presence and active participation of the faithful, *this way of celebrating them is to be preferred* to a celebration that is individual and quasi-private. (*CSL,* Art. 27)

Seen in this way the celebration of the liturgy, and especially the celebration of the Mass, becomes a living manifestation of what the Church really is, a priestly society, a worshipping community. Hence the importance of the

Sunday parish Mass, not just as a means for the individual to fulfill his obligation but as the manifestation, the sacrament, of the Church itself. Each authentic liturgical assembly, truly communal, is a local manifestation of the full assembly of the saints described in the Apocalypse and the Epistle to the Hebrews. It is the earthly reflection of the festive throng about the throne of God and in the sight of the Lamb.

> But you are come to Mount Zion, and to the city of the living God, the heavenly Jerusalem and to innumerable angels in festive gathering, and to the assembly of the first born who are enrolled in heaven, and to the spirits of just men made perfect, and to Jesus the mediator of the new covenant. . . . (Heb 12,22ff)

In the measure that the real parish assembly here on earth approaches this ideal we can say that it is fulfilling its role of being a sign uplifted in the sight of the nations, that it is realizing the gospel ideal of the city upon the mountain that cannot be hid. The way the parish celebrates the Sunday Mass is the standard of its effectiveness in the world. If the Mass does not show us how to live and how to love, there is something wrong with our eucharistic devotion, something lacking in our understanding of what the Mass is.

THE MASS RITE

In keeping with what we have just said about looking at the eucharistic celebration as a whole, we will devote this section to a general view of the Mass, tracing its development broadly from apostolic times to our own day. At the same time we will try to show how the Mass rite itself gives us a precious insight into the sacrament of the eucharist. The sections that follow will attempt a synthesis of the doctrine of the eucharist as sacrifice, sacrament, and sacrificial sacrament.

The Mass of the Roman rite as it is celebrated today falls into two distinct, if related, divisions. Roughly speaking, the first part centers around the book and the second part around the bread and wine. One is the service of the word, the other the eucharistic service. In the immediate past these parts have been known as the Mass of the Catechumens and the Mass of the Faithful. But these terms are inexact, to say the least. They imply that the first part of the Mass is reserved for the nonbaptized, which is not true and never was. Furthermore, they give the impression that the sole purpose of this part is to impart instruction. That is not true either, for even today this first part has prayers and chants as well as readings.

Even less satisfactory, if not downright unfortunate, is the term "fore-Mass" to designate the first part. This term implies a prelude or a foreword to the main event, which is not really part of that event. It encourages people to view the earlier portion lightly and not to worry much about missing it. The *Constitution* takes a much more meaningful approach to these divisions: "The two parts which, in a certain sense, go to make up the Mass, namely, the liturgy of the word and the eucharistic liturgy, are so closely connected with each other that they form but one single act of worship." (Article 56) In other words they are not independent of each other. Each has the same basic function, which is to be—each in its own way—a part of the liturgy. They contribute to one another and together make up one single act. What is proclaimed in the liturgy of the word is celebrated in the eucharistic liturgy. We are right in saying that the liturgy of the word is also a celebration, whereas the liturgy of the eucharist is also a proclamation. The whole action is at once celebration and proclamation. "As often as you eat this bread and drink the cup of the Lord you proclaim the death of the Lord until he comes." (1 Cor 11,26)

Christ appears and is present in both parts of the Mass, although in different ways and to different degrees. In the one he is present in his word, which at the same time is his action; in the other he is present in his action, which becomes a reality through the word that he speaks.

The Liturgy of the Word

The liturgy of the word dates from apostolic and even pre-Christian times. It is the legacy of Jewish synagogue worship to the Christian Church. This synagogue service was of immense importance in keeping the religious ideals of Israel alive in the Graeco-Roman world. Every city of the Roman Empire and many of the towns and villages had at least one synagogue, where on the Sabbath devout Jews and "God-fearing" gentiles gathered to hear the word of God, to pray and to sing his praises.

The service was simple and devotional. First there was the *Shemoneh Esreh,* a series of prayers. Then the scroll of the Torah was brought from the ark to the lectern. During this procession (similar to our gospel procession at solemn Mass) a series of prayers and responsories was said or sung. There came readings from the Pentateuch or Book of Moses, followed by a eulogy of the Book of the Law; then there were readings from the prophets, followed by a commentary. After the address came prayers of intercession said by all for various intentions. At the end of the prayers the cantor returned the Book of the Law to the ark. The people then sang Psalm 2, and with this song the morning prayer ended.

We see Jesus himself, and later his apostles, taking part in such a service. St. Luke gives an account of Jesus in the synagogue at Nazareth reading the Book of Isaia from the scroll that was handed to him, and commenting on the text: "The Spirit of the Lord is upon me. . . ." The apostles Paul and Barnabas went to the synagogue at Antioch and after the reading from the Law and the prophets were invited to discourse to the people.

So we have as the elements of this synagogue service: reading from

79

the Scriptures—"the Law and the prophets"; what we would call a sermon; and finally intercessory prayers.

The first Christians were Jews who continued their participation in this synagogue service until they definitely broke with Judaism. Even then, they did not abandon this service altogether; they transferred it to their own liturgical gatherings. However, they did not leave it unchanged, but added the Christian Scriptures to the Old Testament readings. The earliest account we have of the Christian Sunday eucharistic gathering appears in the first *Apology* of St. Justin Martyr about A.D. 150.

> On that day which is named after the sun, all those who live in the city and the country come together, and then the memoirs of the Apostles [that is, the gospels] or the writings of the prophets are read as long as there is time. When the reader has finished, the president makes an address, in which he earnestly admonishes us to practice the beautiful lessons we have just heard. Then we all rise and pray [for one another]. (*First Apology* I, 66)

Here we see the basic Jewish synagogue service transformed into a Christian service. We can also readily recognize, with one major change, the order of our own liturgy of the word: the reading from the Scriptures, the sermon, and in a modified form, the prayers. This similarity will give us a clue to the meaning of this part of the Mass. Because it comes basically from the Jewish service it has the same purpose as that did. The Jews gathered together to hear the word of God, to pray, and to praise God. Therefore the first part of our Mass is a liturgy of the word, with the proclamation of the word in reading and sermon predominating.

We can draw another conclusion from this: The readings are to be proclaimed and heard. We are dealing here with a *service* presided over by someone with authority, a service with action and reaction; we do not simply *hear*, we *respond* to what we hear in chants that follow the reading. It is an articulated service in which each has his part to play. The lector (or subdeacon in the solemn Mass) reads the first reading or epistle, the priest (or the deacon in the solemn Mass) reads the gospel. The choir sings (or the people sing or say) the entrance song, the gradual, and the alleluia verse, and the people sing the "Lord, have mercy" and the "Glory to God" (or recite them at low Mass).

There are two readings (epistle and gospel) on Sundays but during the week there are sometimes three or more. These are usually chosen for their appropriateness to the season of the liturgical year or to the feast that is being celebrated. In the early Church they usually continued from where they had ended the previous Sunday. But whatever they are, the purpose of the readings is to proclaim the word of God, that is, to tell in God's own words what he has done. The climax of the readings is the gospel, the good and glad news of salvation. We are to hear this word and to accept it with faith, allowing it to remain with us and bear fruit.

The *Constitution* says that "in the liturgy God speaks to his people and Christ still proclaims his gospel." (Article 33) The readings from Scripture do not merely describe past events; they proclaim present realities. The gospel narratives of healing, driving out demons, and raising the dead, for example, tell what is going on now in the Church. The words of Christ and the apostles: "Seek you first the kingdom of God" (Mt 6,33), or, "Walk as children of the light" (Eph 5,8), are directed to us in this time and place.

In the course of time prayers (for example, the collect) and chants (for example, the entrance song) were added to the original structure of the Mass. These chants were usually taken directly or indirectly from the Scriptures and especially from the Book of Psalms. The "Glory to God," for example, is a hymn which begins with a sentence of the gospel and then develops that sentence in the language and style of the psalms. The entrance song is intended to set the tone for the entire celebration. The "Lord, have mercy" is an invocation to the risen Christ, the *"Kýrios,"* begging him to save and to set free. The gradual was originally a responsorial chant, a kind of musical response to the words of the epistle. The alleluia accompanies the gospel procession and is itself a one-word hymn of praise to God (alleluia means "praise God"). The creed is the solemn profession of faith: "the hymn of the faithful." The collect, as its name indicates, collects the prayers of the faithful, summarizes them, and offers them to God.

The sermon which concludes the liturgy of the word should as a rule be a commentary on and an application of the Scripture texts. It is intended to be organically connected to the Scripture readings and chants. This traditional view of the function of the sermon at Mass has been reaffirmed by the *Constitution* in two places.

> The sermon . . . should draw its content mainly from scriptural and liturgical sources . . . a proclamation of God's wonderful works in the history of salvation, the mystery of Christ, ever made present and active within us, especially in the celebration of the liturgy. . . . The sermon is part of the liturgical service. (Article 35,ii)
>
> By means of the homily, the mysteries of the faith and the guiding principles of the Christian life are to be expounded from the sacred text, during the course of the liturgical year; the homily therefore is . . . part of the liturgy itself. (Article 52)

The idea is that the sermon, or homily, is not an interruption of the Mass but rather an integral part of it, making the necessary transition from the liturgy of the word to the eucharistic liturgy. It is part of the whole celebration; that is why it should normally be given by the celebrant.

We can see from this necessarily brief survey that the "liturgy of the word" is not intended merely to instruct. It is in no sense of the word a "class," not even a religion class. The purpose of classroom instruction is to teach; the purpose of the liturgy of the word is to pray. It is a celebration of what God has done for us so that we may be able to respond to that by sacrifice in the second part of the Mass. Worship is not something that we do for God, it is our response to what God has done for us. But in order to respond properly we must know what God has done and we must recall it to mind frequently. This is one of the functions of the liturgy of the word. It is supposed to arouse our faith and our devotion so that we may participate more fervently in the sacrificial action. Sacrament and word go together. They are not in opposition to one another but complement and complete one another. The word is the commentary on the action of the sacrament. The sacrament seals the truth expressed by the word. The sacrament would be unintelligible without the clarifying explanatory word that precedes it, just as the word would be unfulfilled without the sacrament.

In the eucharistic sacrifice we neither see Christ nor hear his voice. That is why we first must hear his voice in the Scriptures that precede it. They give us that detailed commentary on the mystery of Christ which enables us to enter fully into the sacrament and encounter Christ. To put it in another way, they enable us to recognize Christ in the eucharist for who he is.

On the other hand, if the only encounter we had with Christ was in the Scriptures, he would still be far from us. We would hear his voice, true, but there would be no contact with his humanity. For that we need the sacraments, but the sacraments as illumined by the faith the word arouses in us.

This is not the only function of the liturgy of the word, however. It exists for its own sake; it too is a celebration, or *eucharistía,* an act of praise and thanksgiving. We have only to think of the prominent place given to prayer in this liturgy of the word to see that this is true. The psalm texts are all prayers of praise or petition; the "Lord, have mercy" is an acclamation of praise to the risen Christ as well as a plea for salvation. The "Glory to God," especially, is a perfect hymn of praise to God the Father and Christ the Redeemer. Even the collect, while primarily a prayer of petition, always starts from a proclamation of what God has done.

Therefore long before we reach the eucharistic liturgy we have been giving praise to God. The whole Mass is eucharistic.

The Eucharistic Liturgy

The second part of the Mass is called the eucharistic liturgy or the liturgy of sacrifice. It takes its name "eucharist" from the great prayer of blessing and thanksgiving that Jesus said at the last supper. *"Giving thanks, he broke the bread and gave it to his disciples."* (Canon of the Roman rite) The apostles continued to use this prayer, "the thanksgiving," "the *eucharistía,"* and made it the central prayer of the Mass. "To celebrate the eucharist" was to take bread and wine, say this prayer over them, and *thus* consecrate and dedicate the bread and wine to God. Eventually the name was also applied to the reserved sacrament.

It is most important that we remember that originally "the eucharist"

82

was the great prayer of thanksgiving; otherwise we will miss an important clue to the whole doctrine of the eucharist, sacrifice and sacrament. The clue lies in the meaning of *eucharistía* itself. It is a Greek word used by the New Testament writers to translate the Hebrew word *beraka,* "blessing." We usually translate *eucharistía* or eucharist as "thanksgiving," which is somewhat misleading. Actually *eucharistía* has many meanings. The root of the word is *cháris,* Greek for gift or grace. *Eu-charis-tía* therefore presupposes a gift or a grace that is given; something beautiful, rich, noble, good, that calls for a *response* from the one who receives it. *"Eu-"* means good and joyful. When combined, the two roots make a new word connoting a joyous *response* to a benefit received.

When speaking of man's return or response to God one must speak at the same time of a spiritual inward response, of the gift of mind and will. God will not be satisfied with any material gift—none of these things is really adequate, for he possesses them all. The only thing God does not possess until we give it back to him is ourselves. The visible sacrifice or offering we make is only the outward sign of that invisible offering. The visible sacrifice is only an outward formality if it does not express the inner offering of heart and will.

The word *"eucharistía"* hardly occurs as such in the Old Testament but the idea is there, expressed in various words: to bless, to confess, to praise, to offer a sacrifice of praise. It is very important to note that all these different words are extensions or amplifications of *"gratias agere"* or *"eucharistía."* All are included in the idea of "giving thanks." Only when we understand and remember this will we be able to understand what thanksgiving, in the liturgical sense, really means. All these different words may be summarized in one sentence: To give thanks is to worship, for worship is the response of loving adoration that the creature makes to the creator.

By using such a variety of words the Scriptures help us to understand what a rich, many-sided activity worship really is.

We approach still closer to complete understanding when we reflect that the only adequate thanksgiving (praise, worship) we can offer God is the sacrifice of his only-begotten Son. Thanksgiving, or *eucharistía,* therefore becomes a synonym for offering sacrifice to God. The invitation *"Gratias agamus Domino Deo nostro,"* "Let us give thanks to the Lord Our God," does not mean praise or worship in general but the *specific* praise and worship we are gathered here to offer. A better translation would therefore be "Let us together offer God the sacrifice of thanksgiving."

The reason why our own Roman eucharistic prayers and the prayers of all the various liturgies ancient and modern use so many words to express this central idea is simple. They are all derived from the same source: the "prayer of blessing" which Jesus said at the last supper, a source itself inspired by the prayer forms used in the Jewish liturgy for centuries before the time of Christ.

83

A Jewish meal was always a religious affair. It opened and closed with prayer. The particular prayer from which all the later Christian prayers derived was a kind of grace after meals. (In this very expression "grace after meals," incidentally, we maintain the original idea of *beraka, eucharistía,* the recognition of a grace bestowed.) But there is an important difference between our grace at meals and the Jewish prayer of blessing. We ask God to bless us and the food. But the Jew blessed *God* for giving the food. His grace before and after meals was a hymn of praise to God—a thank-offering and at the same time a prayer that God would continue to bestow this food and all his blessings upon his people. The prayer concluded with a prayer for Israel, Jerusalem, Mt. Zion, and for the kingdom of David.

This blessing was therefore a hymn of praise to God for all he had done for his people, for the blessings of creation and deliverance, for the covenant, and for the promised land. As we shall see, the Christian Church continued to make this prayer, adding to the thanksgiving (or blessing) for the creation and the deliverance, a thanksgiving for the blessings of the redemption, the new covenant, the sending of the Spirit, and the eternal glory of heaven which the death of Christ secured for us.

In summary, we call this part of the Mass the eucharistic liturgy because during it we offer God the sacrifice of praise, thanksgiving, and worship. We do this through the medium of a great prayer which glorifies and praises God, which worships him and gives thanks to him for what he has done. It is a prayer that dedicates, offers, and consecrates to God the bread and wine, which he accepts and by the power of the Spirit transforms into the body and blood of his Son. This bread and wine thus becomes "the eucharist" in concrete form, the living praise and glorification of his heavenly Father. Through this same prayer we join our sacrifice to Christ's; more precisely his sacrifice becomes the vehicle of our praise (*eulogía*), for "By him and with him and in him is to God the Father, in the unity of the Holy Spirit, *all honor and glory.*"

The eucharist is therefore an action prayer, an action in the form of a prayer, and a prayer in the form of an action. It is the joyful response that the Church makes to God for all that he has done. It is a sacrifice, for it is an offering to God of the perfect worship, praise, and thanksgiving that the Son of God once made upon the cross. It is a sacrifice, too, because in offering Christ's sacrifice the Church offers herself and all of us in union with him.

THE GREAT EUCHARISTIC PRAYER   The central part of the Mass is the great eucharistic prayer during which the bread and wine are offered to God and consecrated, becoming the body and blood of Christ. For that reason, this prayer is known as the consecration prayer, the one that offers sacrifice to God. In spite of its discontinuous appearance in the modern Roman missal, we must remember that it is in reality one single, unbroken prayer, beginning with the dialogue before the preface and ending with the doxology and the *Amen* of the people.

84

The eucharistic prayer is divided into two parts: one recited aloud, consisting of the preface and sanctus, the other recited in a low tone (except in cases of concelebration) and now called the canon. Originally, however, the *whole* prayer was called the canon, and was recited aloud from beginning to end until the seventh century if not later.

The word "canon" is Greek for measuring-rod or carpenter's rule. The full phrase is *canon actionis,* "the norm or standard for the sacred action," *"gratiarum actio." "Actio"* was in fact one of the names for the eucharistic prayer in former times. Other names were *"oratio"*—prayer; *"prex"*—prayer; and *"praefatio"*—solemn prayer. The original name was *"eucharistia."* The Eastern rites call it the *"anáphora,"* prayer of offering.

The Roman eucharistic prayer, the preface and canon, is the product of a long development that began in apostolic times. It assumed its present form during the fifth century. We have no complete text of this prayer from apostolic times but there are echoes of it in the Apocalypse and in very early Christian literature.

St. Justin does not give the text in the earliest description of the Mass that has come down to us, but he does give us an idea of what it is like. What he has to say about the eucharistic liturgy in general is of supreme importance for us.

> Then, bread and a chalice containing wine mixed with water are presented to the one presiding over the brethren. He takes them and offers praise and glory to the Father of all, through the name of the Son and of the Holy Spirit, and he recites lengthy prayers of thanksgiving to God in the name of those to whom he granted such favors. At the end of these prayers and thanksgiving, all present express their approval by saying "Amen." This Hebrew word, "Amen," means "So be it." And when he who presides has celebrated the eucharist, they whom we call deacons permit each one present to partake of the eucharistic bread and wine and water; and they carry it also to the absentees . . . and, as we said before, after we finish our prayers, bread and wine and water are presented. He who presides likewise offers up prayers and thanksgivings, to the best of his ability, and the people express their approval by saying "Amen." The eucharistic elements are distributed and consumed by those present, and to those who are absent they are sent through the deacons. The wealthy, if they wish, contribute whatever they desire, and the collection is placed in the custody of the president. (*First Apology* I, 66)

We can see from this that the sacrificial action is expressed by means of a prayer and that this prayer is one of praise and honor to God the Father, through the Son and in the Holy Spirit. The motive for giving thanks or praise is "because we have been made worthy by him to partake of these gifts." We can recognize in this the outline, at least, of our preface-canon, with its prayer of praise and thanksgiving for the redemption, its consecration formula followed by *anámnēsis,* its prayer for fruitful communion and concluding doxology. One big difference, however, appears immediately: the prayer described by St. Justin is a spontaneous composition by the president (the bishop). He follows a certain pattern but the exact wording is left to him. This practice was to continue for some time, until the texts began to be written down.

The first complete text of a consecration prayer is contained in the *Apostolic Constitution* of Hippolytus (third century). This prayer begins to approximate our own preface-canon. There is a set form but it is still optional. The bishop is free to use this form or any other "so long as it is orthodox."

The dialogue, only slightly different from ours, begins the prayer; then the bishop continues:

> We give you thanks, O God, through your beloved servant, Jesus Christ, whom in the last times you sent us to be a savior and a redeemer and the messenger of your counsel, who is your Word inseparable from you, through whom you made all things and in whom you were well pleased; whom you sent from heaven into the virgin's womb, and who, conceived within her, was made flesh and demonstrated to be your son, being born of the Holy Spirit and a virgin; who, fulfilling your will and preparing for you a holy people, stretched forth his hands for suffering that he might release from sufferings those who have believed in you.
>
> Who when he was betrayed to voluntary suffering, that he might abolish death and rend the bonds of the devil and tread down hell and enlighten the righteous and establish the ordinance and demonstrate the resurrection, taking bread and making eucharist to you said, Take, eat, this is my body which is broken for you. Likewise also the cup saying, This is my blood which is shed for you. When you do this, you do my *anámnēsis*.
>
> Doing therefore the *anámnēsis* of his death and resurrection we offer you the bread and the cup, making eucharist to you because you have bidden us stand before you and minister to you as priests.
>
> And we pray that you would send your Holy Spirit upon the oblation of your holy Church and would grant it to all the saints who partake to be united to you, that they may be filled with the Holy Spirit for the confirmation of your faith in truth, that we may praise and glorify you through your beloved servant, Jesus Christ, through whom honor and glory be to you with the Holy Spirit in your holy Church, now and forever and world without end. Amen.

This is a fine example of what the eucharistic prayer should contain. We notice that it is not interrupted in any way, that it is direct and to the point, moves on steadily to the end, and finally, is brief. We can see many resemblances to our own canon: the preface, the words of consecration, the *anámnēsis*, the prayer for fruitful communion, the doxology.

Sometime between this prayer of Hippolytus and the fourth century, our own prayer began to take shape. The prayer of Hippolytus was in Greek, but the oldest fragment of what we must regard as the immediate ancestor of our prayer is in Latin. We find this fragment in the treatise of St. Ambrose *On the Sacraments*. It represents the central part of the eucharistic prayer as it was said at Rome and Milan in the last part of the fourth century. Similar to our canon, it is still rather crude and rough-hewn. It lacks the greater elegance and rhetorical beauty of the present Roman canon.

The first complete text of the eucharistic prayer of the Roman Church appears in the Gelasian Sacramentary, or Mass-book, of which a good part goes back to the fifth century. We can safely say that, with some slight changes, this was the form the prayer had reached by the year 500.

Already it had acquired the characteristics of the modern preface-canon: the variable preface and the Holy, Holy, Holy in the text as we know it today. We can see that a deliberate effort has been made to give it the rhetorical style of a public speech. Obviously, too, it was meant to be said aloud. Only the custom of ornate renderings of the sanctus—not substantial theological reasons—reduced the canon to silence. It does not make much sense that the chief prayer of the Mass, with all its references to the Mass as the sacrifice of the Church, should be said so that no one can hear it, or hearing it not understand it. Examination of the text will show that it is intended to stir up the faith and devotion of the people as well as that of the celebrant.

Finally, it is an anomaly that the essential "form" of the sacrament of the eucharist should be said silently, whereas all the other sacramental forms must be audible. What results is that one-half of the sign—the words—is not perceived by those who should hear them. In that way the eucharistic sign itself is to a large extent frustrated.

A growing awareness of the importance of the word in all of the sacraments is bound to result eventually in a more meaningful arrangement. Meanwhile, tradition is strong and authorities are usually reluctant to change what has been the accepted practice for over a thousand years.

The second-century description of the Mass tells us that "bread and a cup of wine mingled with water are brought to the president of the brethren." (St. Justin, *First Apology*, 66–67) Later this rite became more elaborate. The bread and wine were brought to the altar in procession, or, as at Rome, the deacons collected the offerings (bread and wine) of the people and after putting aside some for the poor, brought the rest to the altar.

During this offertory procession, the choir sang the offertory hymn which was a psalm with a refrain called the antiphon. The psalm was gradually eliminated but the term "antiphon at the offertory" in our modern Roman missal preserves the memory of this ancient "offertory."

The essential significance of the offertory was that the people presented the bread and wine for the sacrifice. Their offering of bread and wine represented themselves and meant that they were offering themslves to God. This is still the essential meaning of the offertory action, but it is made more evident when the bread and wine is presented by representatives of the congregation. This helps to illustrate the active part that the people have in the Mass.

On the other hand, the significance of the offertory should not be exaggerated. It is in no sense a sacrificial action by itself. The real offering takes place during the canon when the bread and wine are effectively offered to God. The offertory rite sets the stage for the sacred action and prepares the material for the sacrifice, but it is not the sacred action itself. It consisted originally of a single prayer recited aloud "over the gifts." A frequent theme is that of the exchange: we give the gifts to God and ask that he give them back transformed into the body and blood of his Son.

During the early middle ages, mostly in the Frankish territories (modern France, Belgium, the Rhineland) many other prayers were added before the *secreta* was reached, with the result that the clean lines of the ancient offertory action became obscured. Future revisions of the Roman missal will, we hope, eliminate these additions and simplify the whole action.

The bread used for Mass must be made of wheat. The wine must be the juice of the grape. For many centuries the bread was leavened bread in the form of large loaves that had to be broken before being distributed. For a number of reasons the Latin rites adopted the use of unleavened bread, one reason being that unleavened bread has the advantage of not making crumbs. On the other hand, the bread is supposed to signify nourishing food, the body of Christ in the form of bread. The value of the sign is greatly diminished when the waferlike material does not look or taste like bread. Those who provide this bread are now promoting the use of whole wheat hosts, which resemble bread more closely. The fact that whole wheat bread is more substantial means that it must be chewed like any other food. Only a mistaken reverence has made us think that there is anything disrespectful about chewing the consecrated bread.

THE DIALOGUE   When all is ready for the sacrifice the priest summons the people to join with him in the great eucharistic action. First he greets them with the ancient formula that always precedes each new development in the Mass, "The Lord be with you." Even from the beginning the community note is struck. The people as a people are involved in this action. It is something that concerns them both individually and as a whole. What they are about to do is what they came together to do as a congregation, under the leadership of the priest.

The answer of the people is also more than a mere formality. It shows the union of mind and heart with the priest. By it they signify their readiness to be associated with him in this action.

Sursum corda, the celebrant says next. "Lift up your hearts, turn your minds upward." This is an invitation to join ourselves to that sacrifice continuously occurring in heaven. It means to fix our affections there, as St. Paul says: "If you be risen with Christ, seek the things that are above (*sursum*), mind the things that are above, not the things that are upon the earth." (Col 3,1f.)

The dialogue reaches its climax in the direct invitation to take part in the action; everything else has been anticipating this. "Let us offer to God the sacrifice"; "let us offer the eucharist"; "let us do what Christ commanded us to do as his memorial." We must give these words their full meaning and make them as real as possible. Again we notice how the community as a whole is involved. The priest is not acting on his own without first securing the wholehearted assent of the people. He is not an isolated figure but the one who presides over a living congregation.

The eucharistic prayer itself is said by the celebrant in the name of the whole assembly. It is in the plural throughout, for the offering is the offering of the whole *plebs sancta* and not of the clergy alone. All together "give thanks"; all together "make memorial." The priest is the congregation's spokesman; even though he does not derive his power to speak from the people, he nevertheless exercises it in their name.

THE PREFACE   Once he has received the assent of the congregation to what he is about to do (*Dignum et iustum est*), the priest begins the eucharistic prayer itself. The link between the dialogue and the prayer appears further in the fact that the priest repeats, amplifies, and develops the last words of the dialogue.

"Preface" in Roman liturgical language does not mean "preface" in our modern sense of introduction or foreword, as, "preface to a book." It means a speech delivered in the presence of someone—what we would call an oration. And in fact the canon *is* a solemn oration, a speech delivered not to men, but to God. *Praefatio* therefore meant a solemn prayer. Originally the name was applied to the whole canon; only with the course of time was it restricted to the opening section.

The canon begins with "It is fitting and proper, it is our duty and our salvation always and everywhere to give thanks, to offer praise and glory to God," and it ends with "by him [Jesus Christ] and with him and in him is to you God the Father Almighty all honor and glory for ages and ages. Amen." These are not two different sets of ideas, but one and the same idea begun in the preface and completed in the doxology. The canon is one prayer and it has one theme: praise and glory to God from beginning to end.

This one guiding theme is developed along these lines: it is fitting to offer the sacrifice of praise, but we can offer that sacrifice only by and through the sacrifice of Christ. That sacrifice is eternally present in heaven. How can we join ourselves to it? Only by re-enacting that one sacrifice here on earth through the rite that he himself left us and told us to perform. Therefore through the ministry of the priest we re-enact the last supper and make Christ's sacrifice present on earth. We make his sacrifice ours, asking the heavenly Father that through communion in that sacrifice we may be filled with every heavenly blessing and grace. We conclude with the summarizing doxology.

The modern prefaces of the Roman rite divide the thanksgiving for the redemption into separate clauses, each dwelling on a single event in the whole redemptive work. Nevertheless this is done in such a way that what-ever *single* event is considered, the preface still views the *whole process* from that particular aspect. The Church always views the redemption as a whole, even though she may stress certain aspects of it according to the feast or liturgical season. The eucharistic prayer is always a thanksgiving for the whole redeeming work of Christ.

The *Sanctus* does not interrupt the canon but rather continues it. It is part of the chorus of praise which the entire eucharistic prayer is by defini-tion. Far from distracting us from the main purpose of the prayer, the point of the Sanctus is to show us that it is through the eucharistic sacrifice that we more effectively join in the hymn of the angelic hosts, a hymn which we must not forget is led by Christ himself.

TE IGITUR   Liturgies other than the Roman pass quickly from the singing of the Holy, Holy, Holy to the narrative of the institution. It seems probable that the Roman rite did so too at one time, but somewhere in the fifth century the Roman authorities inserted a series of intercessions and commemorations at this point.

The prayer *Quam oblationem* which forms the immediate introduction to the words of consecration is one of the oldest parts of the canon and asks that God may transform these elements of bread and wine so that our human offering becomes the sacrifice of Christ. "Bless this offering, O God, approve and ratify it and make it an acceptable and spiritual sacrifice so that it may be for us the body and blood of Christ."

The text of the narrative of the institution is not taken verbatim from the Scriptures, though of course it gives the substance of what we find in the synoptics and chapter eleven of 1 Corinthians. A comparison of what we have now in the missal and the most ancient fragment of the canon shows that the form has been adorned and embellished by phrases which, although they are from the Scriptures, do not occur in the account of the last supper.

We should also remember that the words of consecration are not in-tended to be a mere historical record. They are part of the eucharistic prayer and are set in the context of the sacrifice. Neither are they to be considered a magic formula. They have the effect our Lord wanted them to have only in the context in which he intended they should be used. With this under-standing we may say that, taken as a whole, the words of consecration tell us everything about the eucharistic sacrifice. It is no exaggeration to say that they contain the whole gospel. The entire Mass and particularly the great prayer is the sign of the eucharist, but these words constitute the very heart of the sign. By examining them in detail we can reach an understanding of the reality they signify.

Take and eat of this, all of you.   The eucharist is not only a sacrifice, it is a sacrificial *meal*. Our Lord intended the eucharist to be food. Communion is an integral part of the eucharistic sacrifice. That is why Catholics are encouraged to receive communion at every Mass they offer. We are not merely to understand the sacrifice of the cross intellectually, with the mind; we are to assimilate it, to take it in and make it our own, which can be done only by eating.

This is my body. The original Aramaic has no verb. It was simply, *This my body.* But the whole context of revelation shows that our Lord meant these words to be taken literally. Only by his being really and wholly present can this bread and wine be what it is meant to be: the sacrament of redemption. Furthermore St. Paul adds "given for you," that is, offered in sacrifice. Some versions of his words give "broken" or "crushed" as alternate forms. The sacrificial implications are clear enough in any case. It is not simply the body of Christ, but the offered, sacrificed, body of Christ. By using the two separate formulas "This is my body," "This is my blood," Jesus was using a device often employed by the prophets, a symbolic gesture which indicated that the body was separated from the blood. That alone would indicate death and sacrifice to Jewish hearers.

Take and drink this, all of you. For this is indeed the cup of my blood . . . Even more clearly than "This is my body," the second phrase indicates that this action is the sign of Christ's sacrifice. During his life he used the word "cup" by itself to indicate his passion. "Can you drink of the cup that I am to drink?" (Mt 20,22) "My father, if this cup cannot pass unless I drink it, thy will be done." (Mt 26,39) The cup is a biblical symbol for the will of God. To drink the cup is to do God's will, therefore "the cup of my blood" signifies the voluntary passion, "obedient to his Father's will."

. . . of the new and eternal covenant. "Moses took the blood, sprinkled it on the people, and said: 'This is the blood of the covenant that Yahweh has concluded with you on these conditions.'" (Ex 24,8)
The old covenant was sealed with blood as a sign of the bond between Yahweh and his people. But the people were not faithful to that agreement. God therefore planned a new covenant that would be immeasurably better than the old. By this covenant a new people of God would be created. This would not be a covenant that would pass away, but an eternal covenant.
The new covenant was inaugurated by Christ in the incarnation and sealed in his blood shed upon the cross. He was himself the new covenant, for in the person of the incarnate Word God and men were joined together as they had never been before.

. . . the mystery of faith . . . . This phrase has been generally much misunderstood. It does not mean, as is so often said, that the eucharist is a mystery accessible only to faith. "Mystery of faith" means here that the

chalice or cup contains the blood that is the sacrament of the whole order of salvation. "Source of salvation" would be a closer translation than "mystery of faith."

. . . *which is poured forth for you and for many for the remission of sins.* "The blood of Christ cleanses from all sin" and so becomes the source of salvation for us. Here is the whole gospel concentrated in a single sentence. This is indeed the good news that "the Son of Man gave himself for us that he might redeem us from all iniquity and cleanse for himself an acceptable people pursuers of good works," as the epistle of the midnight Mass of Christmas says. (Ti 2,14) *For you and for many* indicates the universality of salvation. The words will be perfectly fulfilled only on the last day. Christ died for all men but all men will attain salvation only at the time of his second coming. Behind the whole sentence stands the figure of the suffering servant; "my servant who will justify many" (Is 53,11), who "bore our iniquities and carried our sorrows." (*ibid.*) Even "poured forth" indicates the abundance of the redemption that the Messia brought and continues to bring.

As often as you shall do this you will be doing it in memory of me. This means in brief that the action of celebrating this meal constitutes a *living* memorial of all that Christ has done for the salvation of the world. It does not mean merely recalling the redeeming work to mind, but *making it present again.* For a Jew "memorial' did not mean reminding one of someone or something that was absent. It meant bringing that person or event back into the present. The memorial was an objective one. The Mass not only reminds us of what Christ has done but also makes him present with all he is and all he has done. Hence it is a *living* memorial. The eucharist makes Christ present as he is, the Lord who has passed through death and now reigns in glory. The Mass makes present again the whole sacrifice of Christ: offered on the cross, accepted in the resurrection, brought into the heavenly sanctuary in the ascension. *In mei memoriam* would be translated better as "making my memorial." Every time we do this we make a living, objective memorial of the passion, resurrection, and ascension.

It is the teaching of the Church that the Mass is not only a sacrifice of thanksgiving but also a propitiatory and impetratory sacrifice as well; that is, it avails us for pardon and grace.

UNDE ET MEMORES . . . After the priest has repeated the words of Christ, using a formula which is a synthesis of St. Paul's words and the words of Christ, "As often as you do this you are doing my memorial," he says "That is why we your servants [the clergy] but also your holy people [the faithful] *making memorial* of the blessed passion, the resurrection from the grave and the glorious ascension, *offer* to your Majesty a sacrificial victim that is pure, holy and undefiled, the holy bread of eternal life and the cup of everlasting salvation." The sacrifice that we offer is the means of making memorial and we make memorial by offering the sacrifice.

The *"Unde et memores"* is not a prayer distinct from the sacrificial action itself—not something appended to it, as it were, but the statement of the meaning of the action. The narrative of the institution gives the reason for what the Church is doing and at the same time *is* what she is doing. It is the "consecration," that is, the making memorial and the offering of sacrifice at the same time.

The ancient eucharistic prayers all began with a thanksgiving to the Father, followed by the *"anámnēsis,"* or "memorial," of the work of Christ. The words of institution were located in the heart of that *anámnēsis.* The eucharistic prayers then concluded with a request that the Holy Spirit come down upon the gifts and upon the community.

We can see that this pattern is followed by the Roman canon. After the "memorial" the priest prays that God the Father will look graciously upon this sacrifice as he looked upon the sacrifices of the Old Law that led up to the sacrifice of Christ, and that he will take it up to the altar on high, joining our sacrifice to the sacrifice that occurs in heaven, so that everyone who receives *from this altar* will be filled with every heavenly blessing and grace. The latter phrase, "blessing and grace," means, of course, above all, the Holy Spirit and the holiness and salvation that he brings.

This is the part of the canon that Pius XII quoted in *Mediator Dei* (1947) when he encouraged priests to distribute communion from hosts consecrated at the same Mass, "from this altar," so that these words would correspond closer to the reality. The *Constitution on the Sacred Liturgy* also says "That more perfect form of participation in the Mass whereby the faithful, after the priest's communion, receive the Lord's body from the same sacrifice, is strongly recommended." (Article 55)

In ancient times the doxology and the end of the canon came at this point. Instead we pray now for the dead and for priests.

The great doxology summarizes the theme of thanksgiving and restates it once again, "By him and with him and in him is all honor and glory forever and ever unto you, God the Father, in the unity created by the Holy Spirit [that is, the Church].

To this and to the whole prayer the people give their assent and join in the sentiments expressed by the priest saying "Amen." This means not "so be it," as Justin mistakenly thought, but "it is" or "it is true!" or "we agree with it." It is a one-word profession of faith and of adherence to the thoughts expressed in the entire prayer.

COMMUNION   Until at least the twelfth or thirteenth century the faithful received communion under two kinds, the consecrated bread from the priest and the consecrated wine from the deacon. In the early Church they stood, held out their hands crossed with palms upward to receive the host, and then communicated themselves. This had the advantage of giving

93

them greater participation in the sacramental act. But with the introduction of unleavened bread this practice was discontinued and the host was placed on the tongue.

In 1964 the Sacred Congregation of Rites restored the ancient formula for holy communion. The celebrant says "The body of Christ," which means the body of Christ that was offered in sacrifice. To this the communicant answers "Amen," which means "It is." It expresses faith in Christ, in the biblical sense of commitment and adherence to the Savior of the world.

After about the twelfth century communion of the faithful under two species was gradually discontinued in the Roman rite. The Eastern rites, with few exceptions, have maintained this practice in one form or another to the present, and it was restored in the West, for certain occasions, in a rite promulgated March 7, 1965. It was (and is) an anomaly that people should be forbidden to do what Christ not only allowed but commanded. The Second Vatican Council therefore has judged it proper to revive this practice, at least for certain occasions. (Article 55) No doubt the number of occasions when this is allowed eventually will be increased.

COMMUNION ANTIPHON   In ancient times the fact that holy communion is itself an act of public worship was clearly illustrated as the people came to communion in procession, singing, and after receiving returned to their places singing. They usually sang psalms and their favorite was Psalm 33, with the refrain "Taste and see that the Lord is sweet, blessed is the man that hopes in him." Even if the people did not sing, the choir did; there was always singing at this point. This is the origin of the communion antiphon.

The instruction of the Sacred Congregation of Rites of September, 1958, has encouraged the revival of this practice of singing on the way to and from the altar, or at least of having psalms and other hymns sung during this time. The reason for this is that holy communion is a communal action and a paschal action, too, for it joins us to the risen Lord. It is a joyful and happy event, not an act of private devotion. Singing at communion emphasizes these truths better than anything else, because singing is at once a sign of joy and a sign of community.

The postcommunion was known as the closing prayer in the ancient sacramentaries. Like the other two short prayers of the Mass, the collect and the prayer over the gifts, it is said by the priest in the name of all. As a rule it asks that the communion we have just received may bear fruit here and now by transforming us into Christ and so bear fruit in the life to come by saving us. The eucharist is not only the living memorial of the paschal mystery but also the pledge of eternal life. It is that *because* it is the living memorial of the paschal mystery.

The priest dismisses the congregation with the formula "Go, the Mass is ended," to which the people respond "Thanks be to God." With this the Mass was ended in the early Church. Any other prayers and rites are later additions.

94

THE EUCHARIST IS A SACRIFICE

The wording of the great eucharistic prayer in all the liturgies indicates clearly, as we have said, that the Mass or the holy eucharist is a true and proper sacrifice. The Mass reproduces the last supper, in which Christ left his beloved spouse, the Church, a sacrifice which commemorates and represents his sacrifice upon the cross in the form of bread and wine. Notice that what is offered in the Mass is not a sacrifice *independent* of the sacrifice of the cross, it *is* the sacrifice of the cross made available to us in another form. The Mass derives all its meaning from the sacrifice of the cross; it is not distinct from that sacrifice in any way: "It is one and the same victim; it is the same [Christ] who offers himself today through the ministry of priests and who once offered himself on the cross; the only difference is in the manner of offering." (Council of Trent, Sess. 22 [September 17, 1562], chapter 2, D940[1743])

The "manner of offering" is *sacramental*. The Mass is the sacrament of the sacrifice of the cross. It is a sacramental sacrifice. "Sacramental" here is not opposed to "real." The Mass is a real sacrifice simply because it is the one perfect sufficient sacrifice made present again through sign. The sign is the sacrificial, eucharistic meal which the Mass renews daily.

We must consider the sacrifice and the sacrament as two complementary aspects of the same reality. We can understand how this can be only by invoking the sacramental principle. This is, as Dom Anscar Vonier says, the *key* to the doctrine of the eucharist. The sacramental principle is that the redemptive incarnation is prolonged and made operative throughout time and space by and through the sacred signs. By means of this sacramental arrangement we are in the presence of the same victim, the same redeeming sacrifice, the same priest, that was offered on Calvary. The death of Christ, indeed, the whole mystery of Christ, is made present and available to us.

> In the divine sacrifice that is enacted in the Mass, the same Christ who on the altar of the cross offered himself once by blood is present and is offered in an unbloody manner . . . The victim is one and the same, who, offering himself now by the ministry of priests, formerly offered himself on the cross; the sole difference is the manner of the offering. (D940[1743])

As the paschal meal which centered around the eating of the paschal lamb was the perpetual memorial of the passover-event, so our Lord commanded that the eucharistic meal should be eaten as a memorial of his own passing out of this world to the Father.

In one of the most beautiful passages in any of her official documents the Church points to the relationship between the paschal meal and the eucharist:

At the last supper, on the night in which he was betrayed, in order to leave his beloved spouse the Church a visible sacrifice as the nature of man demands, declaring himself a priest forever according to the order of Melchisedech he offered his body and blood under the species of bread and wine to God the Father and he gave his body and blood under the same species to the apostles to receive, making them priests of the New Testament at that time. This sacrifice was to re-present the bloody sacrifice which he accomplished on the cross once and for all. It was to perpetuate his memory until the end of the world. His salutary power was to be applied for the sins which we daily commit. He ordered the apostles and their successors in the priesthood to offer this sacrifice when he said, "Do this as a memorial of me" (Lk 22,19; 1 Cor 11,24) as the Catholic Church has always understood and taught. *For after he celebrated the old Pasch, which the assembly of the children of Israel offered as a memorial of the passage from Egypt* (Ex 12,1) *Christ* instituted a *new Pasch.* He himself was the new Pasch to be offered by the Church through her priests under visible signs *as a memorial of his passage from this world to the Father* when by the shedding of his blood "he snatched us from the power of darkness and transferred us into his kingdom." (Council of Trent, Sess. 22, chapter 1, D938[1740f]. Italics added).

Theologians have resorted to many theories to explain this mystery, but the real explanation lies in the simple words of the gospel as the Council of Trent rephrases them. The eucharist represents the sacrifice of the cross in both senses of the word "represent": to signify, and to make present again.

The Christ of glory and the Christ of the eucharist are the same. It is the same Christ but the manner of being present is different. We cannot repeat this too often, for the simple reason that when we forget this traditional Christian approach to the mystery we invite trouble, particularly when we try to discover the essence of the sacrifice of the Mass. But if we remember that the victim and priest are the same Christ our Lord, it is not too difficult to see that the essence of the sacrifice is re-produced in the rite of double consecration. This rite both signifies and effects the *sacramental* shedding of Christ's blood. At the consecration of the Mass the body and blood of Christ are sacramentally separated, *in signo* and *in mysterio.* Christ becomes a sacrificial victim as he did on the cross. The words of the secret prayer of the ninth Sunday after Pentecost are verified: "As often as the commemoration of this victim is celebrated the work of our redemption is accomplished."

There is no physical immolation in the Mass. Christ does not die again, nor is he put to death again. There is a real immolation, all the same, for his one perfect immolation that perdures in heaven is rendered present through a kind of dramatization.

What we do on earth is the counterpart of what Christ continues to do in heaven. We do not see our eternal High Priest, we cannot catch any sound of his unending hymn of praise to God the Father. But we can see and hear him by faith in the symbols of his death and resurrection which lie before us on the altar.

THE SACRIFICE OFFERED
ON THE CROSS

What is a sacrifice and why was Christ's death upon the cross the perfect sacrifice? We find the answers to these questions not in some abstract definition of sacrifice but by studying what revelation has to tell us of the meaning of that term. The biblical images are the most satisfactory source of instruction. The etymology of the word is *sacrum facere,* to make holy, that is, to consecrate something or someone to God; to offer it to him, thereby making a gift of it to him. Basically this is the concept of sacrifice found, and continually refined, in both Testaments. The main point of the biblical teaching is that for a sacrifice to mean anything it must come from within. The sacrifice that is acceptable to God is the contrite and humble heart. What he wants is not the gift but the giver.

Nevertheless, ritual sacrifices played a necessary part in the divine pedagogy. They prepared men to accept the idea of the true sacrifice that includes the whole man, outward and inward. They also provided us with the vocabulary of worship without which the New Testament doctrine of the sacrifice of Christ would be incomprehensible. These Old Testament sacrifices were a "shadow of the good things to come."

It is important to note that in these sacrifices, which involved the killing of animals, the *giving* of the animal to God, not its *destruction,* was of importance. The blood of the victims sprinkled on the mercy seat symbolized not death but life, a life surrendered and offered to God. Death as such can never be pleasing to God. It is what death represents, namely, unselfish love, which pleases him.

But how could unredeemed man ever hope of his own power to offer an acceptable sacrifice? The answer of course is that he could not. God himself would have to provide that perfect sacrifice by sending one who was capable of making it. We find that this was God's intention all along. Abraham was speaking wiser words than he knew when he told Isaac, "God will provide the sacrifice, my son." This is brought out with stunning clearness in Psalm 39[40], which Hebrews puts in the mouth of Christ:

> Sacrifice or oblation you wished not
> But ears open to obedience you gave me.
> Holocausts and sin offerings you sought not.
> Then said I, "Behold I come; in the written scroll
> It is prescribed for me:
> To do your will, my God, is my delight,
> And your law is within my heart." (Ps 39 [40], 7ff)

97

Here at last is the perfect sacrifice, a life given and consecrated to God, the sacrifice of an obedient will. This is the interior and spiritual sacrifice that far surpasses and transcends the most spiritual sacrifices of the Old Law. In Christ, obedient even to death, and the death of the cross at that, God has provided the acceptable sacrifice.

In addition to the ritual sacrifices demanded by God in the Old Law there are others which prefigured that of Christ and prepared the way for it. Three of these are mentioned every day in the canon of the Mass—the sacrifices of Abel, Abraham, and Melchisedech.

The canon calls Abel "just [that is, righteous] Abel." He is the type of innocence and sinlessness. He offered the firstborn of his flock and their fat portions. His offering was a generous one, and he paid for his generosity with his life. In all these respects the figure of Abel is a vague foreshadowing of Christ.

The figure of Abraham, on the other hand, stands out clearly. He is the ancestor of Israel and the spiritual ancestor of us all. His sacrifice has much more significance than Abel's, for he stood to lose more by it. He had been promised an heir and an inheritance. In his descendants all the nations would be blessed, God had told him. Yet he was told to sacrifice, to put to death, the one human hope he had for any posterity. He entrusted the matter to God and so passed the test of faith. God sent his angel to stay his hand from slaying his only son. It was a real sacrifice, though no blood was shed.

Abel's sacrifice recalls the death of Christ. Abraham's sacrifice, with its happy issue, recalls the resurrection—the acceptance of Christ's sacrifice. For that reason the sacrifice of Melchisedech, an offering of bread and wine without violence or slaughter, is considered in a special way to recall our Lord's ascension.

One more Old Testament figure of the sacrifice of Christ remains to be considered: the sacrifice of the paschal lamb. In his gospel St. John is at great pains to bring out the teaching that Jesus is the true paschal lamb. St. Paul says: "Christ our passover [lamb] was immolated." The Church in her liturgy has not only sanctioned this association but reinforced it.

The paschal lamb is intimately involved with the whole exodus-event, even though the custom of killing a yearling lamb and offering it as a springtime sacrifice probably long antedated the exodus. The interest for us is in the special use that was made on that occasion of this primitive rite.

The rite of the passover was to be observed every year as a perpetual ordinance for the Hebrews and their descendants. This day, the day the Lord spared them and led them out of Egypt, was to be "commemorated and solemnized as a feast forever." (Ex 12,14; 13,3–9) The meal was to be a commemorative sacrifice. By eating it the Jew would in a sense share in the experience of his ancestors. "On this day you shall explain to your son this is what the Lord did for *me* when I came out of Egypt." (Ex 13,8)

"Christ our paschal lamb is immolated," St. Paul says, "therefore let us keep festival!" (1 Cor 5,7f) Keep festival because Christ has died for us? Yes, because his death is the sacrifice for our *deliverance*.

> It is fitting and right, our duty and our salvation, always and everywhere to proclaim you gloriously but especially on this night in which Christ our passover was immolated. For he is the true paschal lamb who took away the sins of the world; who by dying destroyed our death and by rising restored life to us. (Preface of Easter)

Throughout his passion Christ stressed that he was in complete control of the situation. He declared that no man could take his life from him; he had power to lay it down and power to take it up again. In the garden he freely accepted the chalice that his Father willed him to drink. When arrested he made no attempt to escape, nor did he try in any way to extricate himself from the peril he was in. Even on the cross he showed that suffering could not degrade or intimidate him, and he died at the moment that he willed to die. His self-offering was complete in every respect.

Because this sacrifice was perfect it contains and summarizes all the praise, all the adoration, all the worship of which the human heart is capable. All other sacrifices have value only to the extent that they resemble this one. Because it is a perfect sacrifice it is capable of accomplishing everything. The obedience of Christ, his self-oblation, cancels out the disobedience of Adam and so reconciles us to God the Father. His sacrifice is able to make full and perfect satisfaction for all the sins of men. Christ's obedient sacrifice cancels out the willfulness that causes sins in others.

How is it possible for us to offer upon our altars the same sacrifice that was offered upon the cross? The answer is simple. We do this by repeating the last supper sacramentally. That, too, was a sacrifice, and for the same reason the Mass is. Jesus offered himself in this supper in the form of bread and wine. The last supper was, in fact, the first act of the passion. Jesus had already decided to offer himself as victim for the world's redemption. He really offered himself, therefore, from that moment onward. His body and blood were already totally given up to his Father's will. The rite that he celebrated and left to his Church as his memorial was a full and complete sacrifice. Every time it is repeated it does what the last supper did—it represents, points to, and signifies, the sacrifice of the cross.

THE EUCHARIST,
THE SUPPER OF THE LORD

In the study of any sacrament our method should be to progress from the sign to the reality signified. It is the full sign that determines the reality there contained. From our study of the Mass we can see that the sign of the   *99* eucharist is a meal. A table is covered with white linen and on it bread and wine are placed. The bread is eaten and the wine is drunk sacrificially, or by way of offering to God. "Take and eat, for this is my body; take and drink, for this is the cup of my blood." The fact that the words are said in the person of Christ shows that Christ is the host at this meal and we are the guests. The meal is therefore not simply a religious meal, it is the Lord's own meal, his supper. The traditional catechesis on the meaning of this action tells us that, "As often as you eat this bread and drink this cup you proclaim the death of the Lord until he comes." The Mass is a meal that is a sacrifice, a sacrifice in the form of a meal.

There is nothing sad about a meal. It is a joyous occasion, a community affair. Even friends who are taking their last meal together greatly enjoy each other's company. Pleasant conversation, kind words, laughter, even on special occasions music and song, add to the enjoyment of a meal.

The Mass is never sad or gloomy. It may be a reverent celebration but it is nevertheless always a celebration. The more celebration there is, the more perfect the sign. A so called "silent" Mass is as much a valid Mass as one celebrated with dialogue and song, but it is a much less perfect sign because it is an imperfect celebration.

If the Mass is a celebration and a meal, what does it celebrate? The Mass is the celebration of the supper of the Lord, the last meal he had with his disciples. This in turn celebrated the pasch in advance, and provided the rite for celebrating it for all time until he comes again. The pasch of the Lord is his passion, resurrection, and ascension, the passage out of the world to the Father. By this passage he accomplished the world's redemption, the return of all mankind to the Father. The Lord's supper is therefore the celebration of our redemption.

We call it the Lord's supper because he is the host at this meal and we are celebrating his victory. Moreover, he is the food we eat. By eating and drinking at the Lord's table we partake of the redemption won for us in his blood. At the same time, because the Lord is Messia, the supper here anticipates the eternal messianic supper hereafter. The eucharist is not only the memorial of the redemption, it is the foreshadowing sign of the final redemption that will be ushered in with the final coming of the Lord.

THE MASS
IS THE SACRIFICE OF THE CHURCH

To say that the Mass is the sacrifice of the Church means not only that the Mass belongs to the Church as her most priceless possession; it means that in and through the Mass the Church offers worship to God and simultaneously offers herself.

Actually it is Christ who offers the sacrifice through the priest who acts in his name. But because the priest is the ordained representative of the

Church, what he does, the Church does. So it is that even when a priest celebrates Mass alone the Mass is still the sacrifice of the whole Church. On the other hand, a churchful of people cannot offer the Mass without the priest.

Ideally, priest and people join in offering the sacrifice together as the canon says: "*nos servi tui* . . . (the clergy) *sed et plebs tua sancta* (the faithful) *offerimus.* . . ." The people do not share directly in the act of consecration but in joining themselves to the priest they thereby truly offer sacrifice. This is clearly brought out in the words of the September, 1958, instruction *On Sacred Music and the Liturgy:*

> By its very nature the Mass requires that all who are present take part in it, each in the way proper to him. *This participation should above all be interior* consisting *in devout attention of mind* and *the affections of the heart.* Thereby the faithful enter into closest union with their high Priest . . . and together with him offer the sacrifice, surrendering themselves in union with him. The participation of those present becomes more complete, however, when in addition to this interior attention there is outward participation manifesting itself in outward acts. (3,22. Italics added).

This same teaching is repeated in the *Constitution on the Sacred Liturgy:*

> Mother Church earnestly desires that all the faithful should be led to that full, conscious, and active participation in liturgical celebrations which is demanded by the very nature of the liturgy. Such participation by the Christian people as "a chosen race, a royal priesthood, a holy nation, a redeemed people" (1 Pet. 2,9; cf. 2,4–5) is their right and duty by reason of their baptism. (Article 14)

> But in order that the liturgy may be able to produce its full effects it is necessary that the faithful come to it with proper dispositions, that their minds should be attuned to their voices and that they should cooperate with divine grace lest they receive it in vain. (Article 11)

By means of and through the eucharistic sacrifice the people offer themselves as victims, holy, living, and pleasing to God. The "acceptable sacrifice" is the eucharistic sacrifice first of all, but that offering must reflect and express the offering of one's whole life. The eucharist is the high point of the offering of our will, mind, heart, affections, our whole self, to God.

It would be a grave error to think that in any way the eucharist dispenses us from interior sacrifice. Our salvation, our death to sin, our return to God, is accomplished once-for-all. Nevertheless, each of us must unite himself to this sacrifice by his personal and free action, by his whole Christian life. We must continue in our lives the return to God inaugurated by Christ, and so complete the redemptive sacrifice on his own account.

101

There is only one sacrifice, just as there is only one Priest. By our baptism we are summoned to continue that sacrifice and make it our own. The eucharist enables us to extend the one sacrifice of Christ into our lives.

Without this true internal participation the Mass does not become *our* sacrifice. Interior participation is by no means opposed to exterior participation. Rightly understood they are two sides of the same coin. The mind must indeed "harmonize with the voice," but to do this voice may not be silent.

We cannot say this too often: the Mass is not a private devotion, it is a community action. The faithful form a community under the leadership of the priest, and because they form one they must act like one. They are a "holy priesthood" and must express this priestliness in some outward way. A community of mute spectators who should be actively involved in the Church's worship is worse than an anomaly; it is a calamity.

THE EUCHARIST—
SACRIFICE AND SACRAMENT OF UNITY

"The sacraments effect what they signify." This basic principle of sacramental theology helps us understand what the effect of the eucharist is in time and in eternity. The eucharist signifies unity and peace; therefore it brings about unity and peace.

Unity is union with God and with one another. It means that all men are gathered together into one household and family, the mystical body of Christ. Peace is first of all reconciliation with God, then the harmony of men with one another. The sacrifice of Christ was directed toward achieving a new bond or alliance between God and man. The sin of Adam had destroyed the harmony and unity that God had established. It had scattered the human race, separating it from God and separating men from one another. Saint John tells us in his gospel that Jesus died "not for the [Jewish] nation only but to gather into one the children of God who were scattered abroad." (Jn 11,51f) Christ came to bring mankind back to God by making mankind one and leading it back to him. Saint Paul is even more explicit about the purpose of Christ's sacrifice:

> But now in Christ Jesus you who were once afar off have been brought near through the blood of Christ. For he is himself our peace; he it is who has made both [Jew and Gentile] to be one, and has broken down the intervening wall of the enclosure . . . that he *might create in himself one new man* and make peace and reconcile both in one body to God by the cross . . . coming, he announced the good tidings of peace both to you who were far off and to those who were near, because through him we both have access in one Spirit to the Father. (Eph 2,13–18. Italics added)

102   The new covenant is essentially a mystery of unity, a unity accomplished first of all in the person of Christ and from him radiating out to all

of us. The purpose of the sacrifice of Christ was to create or reconstitute a new people of God, the true "Israel of God" (Gal 6,16), united to him by the closest of bonds. Foreshadowed in the people of the old covenant, this becomes a reality in the Church of Christ.

In that way the restoration of the human race is accomplished. Through the blood of Christ we now have access in one Spirit to the Father and are united "in one body." Incorporation into Christ, reconciliation with God, union with God and with one another—all this has been accomplished. The unity brought about by Christ is directed to the integral restoration of all humanity, the whole company of the redeemed, around the throne of God, for eternity.

This is the doctrine of the Council of Trent, aimed at those who denied that the Mass was a real sacrifice. The same council also says that our Lord left his beloved spouse, the visible Church, a sacrifice,

> by which there should be represented the sacrifice that was to be offered once by blood on the cross. For having celebrated the Passover supper of the old law, he instituted a new pasch, namely, himself, to be immolated under visible signs by the Church as a memorial of his passage from the world to the Father. (*Ibid.*, chapter 1)

Even though this unity *has been* accomplished, it still *remains* to be accomplished. It has been achieved in principle, but remains to be done for every man who comes into the world until the end of time. Each one must be brought into and maintained in this unity which exists before him and independently of him.

Baptism brings him into this unity but he is maintained in it by the eucharist. Through the eucharist the Church is still in the process of "becoming what she is." The building-up of the body of Christ is a work that is never completed until we reach the "mature measure of the fullness of Christ." (Eph 4,13) The Church's future always lies before her.

The means of the Church's growth is the holy eucharist, the sacrament of charity. The source of all development is the paschal mystery whereby we become ever more assimilated to Christ in his death and resurrection; and the eucharist is the great sacrament of the paschal mystery.

THE EFFECTS
OF THE EUCHARIST

The eucharist makes the cross present and operative among us. The effects of the cross are many but they can be summarized in one: it builds up the Church, that is, makes it holy. Christ died upon the Cross to *create* the Church, to make it holy and spotless, to reconstitute the new people of God. "Husbands, love your wives, as Christ loved the Church and delivered himself up for her that he might sanctify her. . . ." (Eph 5,25)

The picture that St. Paul presents here is the state of the Church as it will be on the last day. The whole life of the Church is a constant move toward the realization of this final goal. What Christ did upon the cross he continues to do in all the sacraments, but especially in the eucharist. That is why we call the eucharist the sacrament of the Church. It makes the Church the Church that Christ wanted her to be.

The Church is a community composed of individual members. In the measure that each of the members is made holy the whole body is made holy. The grace of the eucharist works upon each member individually to bring all to full stature in Christ. Holy communion makes us holy by transforming us into the likeness of Christ, by making us live in him and him in us. We are to present ourselves as victims; living, holy, and pleasing to God. This is our spiritual service: to be conformed not to this world but to the will of God, as Christ was. Basically, therefore, the great effect of the eucharist is to make each of us what Christ is: a son of God.

We cannot do this of ourselves, nor is the grace of baptism and confirmation enough to accomplish it. In order to become sons of God we must be more intimately associated with the sacrifice of Christ. The real reason why we must approach the eucharist frequently is to renew and intensify our relationship with Christ in the sacrament that contains his sacrifice. The eucharist constantly reactivates and renews the life that is in us from baptism. Every communion is a renewal of our baptism and our confirmation.

Holy communion is the application of the incarnation and the redemption to each individual. It is a personal encounter with Christ crucified and risen. Christ comes into each life to bring the power of his grace to bear upon it and to further the work of the redemption. In each one of us the gospel events come to life again, as it were. The healing of the blind man, the raising of the dead, the cure of the lame man, all these happen now to us in another way. "The blind see, the lame walk, the dumb speak, the lepers are cleansed, and dead are raised to life." Once again, as in the days of his mortal life, power goes forth from Jesus and cures all. That is why the communion antiphon so often is a sentence from the gospel such as, "I went and I washed and I saw and I believed in God" (communion song, Wednesday of fourth week of Lent), or "Jesus cried: Lazarus, come forth! And he that was four days dead came forth with feet and hands still bound" (communion song, Friday of fourth week of Lent). This is a way of showing that the good Jesus did to those he met in Palestine long ago he is still doing through the eucharistic mystery.

The final result of the eucharist is to divinize us by making us like Christ. It transforms us into the likeness of Christ. His thoughts become our thoughts, his attitudes, ours. As human friendship tends to make friends resemble one another, share the same views, and understand and sympathize with one another, so the friendship of Christ, maintained and deepened by the eucharist, makes us resemble Christ. It maintains in us the filial attitude of Christ toward his heavenly Father and his fraternal attitude toward our fellow men. Because it brings us in direct contact with the mystery of our salvation it cleanses and purifies us from sin and the effects of sin.

> Participation in the body and blood of Christ effects nothing less than our passing into what we receive. It causes us to carry in our spirit and flesh Him in whom and with whom we are dead, buried, and rise again. (St. Leo, *Sermon* 63)

The final goal of the eucharist is the final goal of the redemptive death of Christ: "to gather together in one the scattered children of God." (Jn 11,52) The Eucharist is therefore the sign of the eschatological unity of the mystical body. St. Thomas gives as the chief effect of the eucharist assembling the Church here with a view to the final assembling hereafter.

> In this sacrament as in all the others, what makes the sacrament what it is is the effect that it produces. Now the sacrament of the eucharist has two effects. The first is to unite us with Jesus Christ, for it contains his body as well as signifying it; the second is to unite us with his mystical body, the society of the saints which it signifies but does not contain. (*S.Th.*, 3,89,4)

The eucharist is the pledge of the resurrection because it joins us to the body of the risen Christ. "He that eats me the same also shall live by me." (Jn 6,58) "I am the resurrection and the life. He that believes in me although he be dead shall live; and everyone who lives and believes in me shall not die forever." (Jn 11,25)

This is the reason why the eucharist in the form of viaticum is pre-eminently the sacrament of the dying. It is called viaticum because it is the food for the journey (*via*) and also the means of conducting us safely to journey's end. Being the foretaste of the messianic banquet, it is the supreme pledge of salvation when received with the proper dispositions. A "sudden and unprovided death" is one in which a person must leave this world without viaticum.

THE REAL PRESENCE

It has always been the faith of the Church that Christ is really present in the sacrament of the eucharist. When we say "really present" we mean that after the words of consecration in the canon, which are the words of Christ, he is present whole and entire ("body, blood, soul—and divinity") in the sacrament of the altar. The bread becomes the body of Christ, the same body which he took of Mary, and which hung upon the cross; the wine becomes his blood, the blood that was shed for us on Calvary. In both species or in either he is wholly and completely present. Whether we receive the bread alone or the wine alone we receive the whole Christ.

The eucharist is the greatest of the sacraments because, whereas the others contain the *power* of Christ, in the eucharist he is present *in person*. He remains present as long as the bread and wine retain the appearance of bread and wine. In the other sacraments he is present as long as the rite of the sacrament lasts. The water of baptism contains the power of Christ while it is being poured on the head, the oil of confirmation contains the power of the passion while it is being used in that sacrament. Once the sacrament has been administered, the water or oil remains blessed but does not itself contain the power of Christ. In the eucharist, however, he is there in person as long as the host remains host, as long as the sacramental wine remains wine.

We cannot prove the mode of presence of Christ in the eucharist except to those who believe the words of Christ and the teaching of the Church. Nothing in the appearance of either the bread or the wine gives us any assurance that Christ is present. We can show that the doctrine is part of the Church's teaching from the beginning, but we cannot prove the truth of it by purely natural reason or arguments.

On the other hand, an examination of the words of Christ and the teaching of the Church will strengthen the faith of those who believe. The words of Christ are clear enough, especially when we put them in the whole context of the revelation of the doctrine. "Take and eat, this is my body." "Take and drink, this is my blood." To take these commands as meaning anything else than they say is to weaken, not only the doctrine of the eucharist, but the doctrine of the incarnation itself. By virtue of the sacrament or the "force of the words," as theologians say, the species of wine contains only the blood. But by virtue of another principle, that of "concomitance," each species contains the whole Christ living, risen, and exalted to the right hand of the Father. This is why communion under either kind is communion in the whole Christ. At the same time, the eucharist is the compendium of all the mysteries of Christ because it contains the incarnate Word in all the states of his life on earth and in heaven.

Any exposition of the Catholic doctrine of the eucharist necessarily involves a reference to the much discussed term "transubstantiation." Like the word *"homooúsios"* to describe the divinity of the Son, this term cannot be found in the Scriptures. But like *homooúsios* it was chosen because at the time it was the best term to express the doctrine, or at least to keep men from making mistakes about it.

The Council of Trent says that "if anyone denies that in the sacrament of the holy eucharist are contained truly, really, and substantially the body and blood together with the soul and divinity of our Lord Jesus Christ, and consequently the whole Christ, but says that he is in it only as in a sign or figure or power [*virtus*] let him be condemned." (Session 13, canon 1) In that same session the council fathers speak of the marvelous conversion of bread into Christ's body and wine into his blood, "which conversion is *rightly* called 'transubstantiation.'" (Session 13, chapter 4)

The term means that the bread and the wine in their entirety are changed, "converted," into Christ in his entirety. Notice that what ·was called "substance" in the medieval period is not annihilated but *converted*. We would say taken over or assumed by Christ, thereby ceasing to be what it had been. Bread and wine are placed in a new relationship to the pre-existing Christ, referred to in his totality as "body and blood." They yield their substance to become his substance, though to the human senses they appear unchanged.

Transubstantiation has the advantage, not of solving the mystery, but of helping us to see how we should think of Christ's presence in the eucharist, and what mistakes we should avoid in speaking of it. We should think of him as present whole and entire, but without the limitations of dimensions, place, or movement. Christ is not *contained* in the bread or in the wine. Such terms as "veiled in the bread" are incorrect because they imply that somehow if you could pull the veil aside you could see him. It would be more correct to say that faith can see him manifested to us by the sign of the foodstuffs. There is no question here of *concealing* anything. The eucharist is a way of *manifesting* Christ's presence, not of concealing it. The real presence in the eucharist is a sacramental one. Christ is there, showing himself in the form of bread and wine. In the days of his mortal flesh he was to be seen as a man. Now he shows himself in the form of bread.

Another consequence of the eucharistic presence is that no injury can be done to Christ there. Nothing that happens to the species affects Christ himself. Nor is he a prisoner in the tabernacle, or contained in it in any way. He is present there but "not as in a place"—not confined, or held, or bound.

Finally, we should refrain from such pious romanticism as speaking of Christ "coming down upon the altar" at Mass. He does not move from one place to another, neither is he in any sense born again sacramentally. We must be content with the simple and sublime reality which faith teaches, that the same Lord who walked this earth, died upon the cross, and now reigns in heaven is present among us in a different manner to be the nourishment of his Church. We should not be distracted from that thought by considerations that have their origin in sentimentality rather than in revealed teaching.

LIVING BY THE EUCHARIST

Holy communion works its effects in us in proportion to our attitude in approaching this sacrament. Since it is of its very nature a personal, intimate encounter with the Savior it demands preparation on our part. We must heighten our receptiveness to the gift, stirring up faith and devotion so that this encounter may be fruitful.

Preparation demands first of all that we be free from serious sin. To receive communion in the state of aversion to God is to deny everything that the holy eucharist represents. If anyone is conscious of the guilt of mortal sin he must go to confession before receiving the eucharist.

Even if we are free from mortal sin we should not go to communion out of custom or habit. The whole Mass rite is calculated to arouse our faith and our love by reminding us that receiving communion is sharing in the sacrifice of Christ and so in his sacrificial dispositions. We should be ready and willing to do what the Lord wishes. Lively faith, ardent hope, sincere love for God and one another, and true sorrow for sin, should mark us inwardly as we approach the table of the Lord. If we make the prayers of the Mass our own prayers we are preparing for communion in the right way.

After we receive communion we should make some kind of thanksgiving, however brief. The Church has provided certain optional formulas of which we can make use. Each one is free to follow his own inclinations in this regard. The important thing is that we try to correspond with the divine gift and pray to do God's will in our lives. Needless to say the first thanksgiving should be the postcommunion prayer, which gives us valuable direction on what the effect of holy communion should be.

The holy eucharist is the supreme sacrament. It is the compendium of all the mysteries of the Christian religion, the living memorial of all God's wonders, the clean oblation, the living bread that comes from heaven, the heavenly antidote against the poison of sin, the immense memorial of God's all-powerful love for us. It is the bond of unity and charity, the refreshment of the saints, the viaticum of those who die in the Lord, and the pledge of future glory. A famous apostrophe attributed to St. Thomas Aquinas, "O sacrum convivium," addresses the holy meal in this way:

"O sacred banquet, in which Christ is received, the memorial of his pasch is celebrated, the mind is filled with grace, and a pledge of future glory is given us!" (Antiphon 2, Vespers of Corpus Christi)

Selected Readings

CHAPTER ONE

Bouyer, Louis, *The Paschal Mystery* (Chicago: Regnery, 1950).

Daniélou, Jean, *Bible and Liturgy* (Notre Dame, Ind.: University of Notre Dame Press, 1958).

Davis, Charles, *Sacraments of Initiation* (New York: Sheed and Ward, 1964).

Diekmann, Godfrey, *Come Let Us Worship* (Baltimore: Helicon, 1961).

Durrwell, F., *The Resurrection: A Biblical Study* (New York: Sheed and Ward, 1960).

Gaillard, J., *Holy Week and Easter* (Collegeville, Minn.: Liturgical Press, 1964).

George, A., *et al.*, *Baptism in the New Testament* (Baltimore: Helicon, 1965).

CHAPTER TWO

Bohen, Marian, *The Mystery of Confirmation: A Theology of the Sacrament* (New York: Herder and Herder, 1963).

Roguet, A. M., *Christ Acts Through Sacraments* (Collegeville, Minn.: Liturgical Press).

Martimort, A. G., *The Signs of the New Covenant* (Collegeville, Minn.: Liturgical Press, 1963).

(The books listed for chapter one are also pertinent to this chapter.)

CHAPTER THREE

Jungmann, Joseph, *The Eucharistic Prayer* (Chicago: Fides Press, 1956).

————, *The Early Liturgy* (Notre Dame, Ind.: University of Notre Dame Press, 1959).

————, *The Mass of the Roman Rite*, 2 vols. (New York: Benziger, 1950-55).

Kilmartin, Edward J., *The Eucharist in the Primitive Church* (Englewood Cliffs, N.J.: Prentice-Hall, 1965).

Masure, E., *The Christian Sacrifice* (New York: Kenedy, 1943).

Parsch, Pius, *The Liturgy of the Mass* (St. Louis: B. Herder, 1957).

Roguet, A. M., *Holy Mass: Approaches to the Mystery* (Collegeville, Minn.: Liturgical Press, 1953).

Delorme, J., *et al.*, *The Eucharist in the New Testament* (Baltimore: Helicon, 1965).

ABBREVIATIONS

The Books of the Old and New Testaments

Genesis	Gn	Canticle of Canticles	Ct
Exodus	Ex	Wisdom	Wis
Leviticus	Lv	Sirach (Ecclesiasticus)	Sir
Numbers	Nm	Isaia	Is
Deuteronomy	Dt	Jeremia	Jer
Joshua	Jos	Lamentations	Lam
Judges	Jgs	Baruch	Bar
Ruth	Ru	Ezechiel	Ez
1 Samuel (1 Kings)	1 Sm	Daniel	Dn
2 Samuel (2 Kings)	2 Sm	Osea	Os
1 Kings (3 Kings)	1 Kgs	Joel	Jl
2 Kings (4 Kings)	2 Kgs	Amos	Am
1 Chronicles (Paralipomenon)	1 Chr	Abdia	Abd
2 Chronicles (Paralipomenon)	2 Chr	Jona	Jon
Ezra	Ez	Michea	Mi
Nehemia (2 Ezra)	Neh	Nahum	Na
Tobia	Tb	Habacuc	Hb
Judith	Jdt	Sophonia	So
Esther	Est	Aggai	Ag
Job	Jb	Zacharia	Za
Psalms	Ps(s)	Malachia	Mal
Proverbs	Prv	1 Machabees	1 Mc
Coheleth (Ecclesiastes)	Coh	2 Machabees	2 Mc

In the enumeration of the Psalms, the first number follows the Vulgate, the number within brackets, the Hebrew text.

St. Matthew	Mt	1 Timothy	1 Tim
St. Mark	Mk	2 Timothy	2 Tim
St. Luke	Lk	Titus	Ti
St. John	Jn	Philemon	Phlm
Acts of the Apostles	Ac	Hebrews	Heb
Romans	Rom	St. James	Jas
1 Corinthians	1 Cor	1 St. Peter	1 Pt
2 Corinthians	2 Cor	2 St. Peter	2 Pt
Galatians	Gal	1 St. John	1 Jn
Ephesians	Eph	2 St. John	2 Jn
Philippians	Phil	3 St. John	3 Jn
Colossians	Col	St. Jude	Jude
1 Thessalonians	1 Thes	Apocalypse	Ap
2 Thessalonians	2 Thes		

Apocrypha and Qumrân Material

Henoch	Hen	Testament of the	
Jubilees	Jub	Twelve Patriarchs	Test
Psalms of Solomon	Ps Sol	Manual of Discipline	MD

Other Source Material

Acta Apostolicae Sedis
[Acts of the Apostolic See]   *AAS*
Ancient Christian Writers,
   ed. J. Quasten and others   *ACW*
Acta Sanctae Sedis
[Acts of the Holy See]   *ASS*
Codex Iuris Canonici
[Code of Canon Law]   *CIC*
Corpus Scriptorum Ecclesiasticorum
   Latinorum
[Body of Latin Ecclesiastical
Writings]   *CSEL*
Denzinger-Schönmetzer,
   Enchiridion Symbolorum, 32d ed.
[Handbook of the Creeds]   *D*
Sacrorum Conciliorum nova
   . . . Collectio   *Mansi*
Patrologia, series graeca,
   ed. J. P. Migne   *PG*

Patrologia, series latina,
   ed. J. P. Migne   *PL*
Rouët de Journel, M. J.
   Enchiridion Patristicum, 21st ed.
[Patristic Handbook]   *R*
Summa contra Gentes
   S. Thomae Aquinatis   *S.C.G.*
Quatuor Libri Sententiarum
   Petri Lombardi [Four Books
of Opinions]   *Sent.*
Summa Theologiae
   S. Thomae Aquinatis   *S.Th.*
Supplementum tertiae partis Summae
   Theologiae (Ottawa ed. 1941)
   Suppl.
The Church Teaches,
   ed. J. Clarkson and others   *TCT*

INDEX

113

Jesus (*Cont.*):
 bread of life, 72 f
 command of, 12 ff
 death of, 30, 32 f, 38, 84
 encounter with, 15
 enlightens us, 8
 incorporation into, 5, 27, 31, 33, 35 f, 66
 mystery of, 1, 19
 resurrection of, 23, 27, 29, 31 ff, 36, 40, 44 f
 sacraments and, 76
 sacrifice of, 76, 89, 91, 93
 sufferings of, 9, 34
 work of, 1, 4, 13
John the Baptist, St.
 baptism of, 9, 11, 16 ff, 55
 baptism of Jesus, 17 f
John, 11, 24, 33, 37 ff, 56, 72 ff, 98, 102
Justin Martyr, St., 80, 85 ff

L

Lent and baptism, 19, 21
Leo I, St., 57, 105
Lighted candle at baptism, 28
Limbo, 44
Liturgy, 4, 14, 19, 77, 81
 of confirmation, 48
 of holy eucharist, 74, 76, 79, 82-85
 purpose of, 81 f
 of the word, 76, 79-82
Luke, 79
Luther, 48

M

Maertens, Dom Thierry, 26
Mark, 9, 12, 16
Martyr, 64
Mass, 77-94, 100 f, 103
 of catechumens, 78
 of faithful, 78
 participation in, 101 f
Matter
 of baptism, 10
 of confirmation, 49, 57
 of holy eucharist, 88
Matthew, 15
Meal-character of eucharist, 3, 70, 74, 76, 90, 99 f
Melchiades, Pope, 51
Melchisedeck, 98
Memorial, eucharist as, 92
Messia, 17, 18, 20, 53, 54, 60
Metaphorical use of "baptism," 9
Minister
 of baptism, 12, 43

of confirmation, 57 ff, 67
Missal, Roman, 19 n, 49
Moses, 29 f, 79, 91
 Canticle of, 24
Mount Zion, 28, 78, 84

N

Necessity of baptism, 42, 44
 of confirmation, 66 f
New Testament, 5, 9, 11, 13, 25, 31, 52, 62, 97
Nicodemus, 11, 37
Noah, 24, 40

O

Old Testament, 10, 13, 15, 24, 52 f, 83, 97
On Sacred Music and the Liturgy, 101
Order in baptism, 148
Order of administration of sacraments, 2, 58 f, 66
 reasons for, 3 f, 66
Order of Holy Week, 23 f
Our Father, 21 f

P

Pasch (of Old Testament), 23
Paschal lamb, 98 f
Paschal mystery, 2, 5, 29, 34, 70, 77
Paul V, Pope, 20
Paul, St., 8, 14, 15, 24, 30, 31-37, 40, 41, 45, 51, 55, 74, 79, 91, 92, 98, 102 f
Pentecost
 baptism on, 12
 confirmation and, 49, 51 f, 61, 62
Peter Lombard, 51
Peter, St. (and *1* and *2 Peter*), 8, 12, 15, 28, 40, 56
Philip, 15, 54, 56
Pius XII, Pope, 93
Place for administering confirmation, 61, 67
Pontifical, Roman, 59
Preface, 89 f
Preparation for communion, 108
Prophets, the, 13
Protestant reformation, 48
Psalms, 81

Q

Queen of Ethiopia, official of, 12

R

Real presence, 105 f
Relation of
  baptism and confirmation, 58, 61 f, 66
  baptism and eucharist, 71
Revelation of doctrine of eucharist, 71 f
Rites
  of baptism, 18 ff, 26, 43
  of confirmation, 49, 56, 59 ff
  "essential," 4
  of eucharist, 76
  of Passover, 98 f
  sacramental, 4
Ritual, Roman, 20, 58
Romans, 15, 31, 38
Rome, 21, 22

S

Sacramental character of confirmation, 48
Sacred Congregation of Rites, 94
Sacrifice
  of Abel, 98
  of Abraham, 97 f
  of the cross, 96, 99, 103
  eucharist as, 95 f, 99-101
  of Melchisideck, 98
  of paschal lamb, 98
  and sacrament, 74 f
Salvation history, 4, 72, 76
Sanctus, 90
Satan
  in conflict with Christ, 30
  renunciation of in baptism, 22, 42
Scriptures, 4, 21, 48, 76, 81, 82
Scrutinies (*See* Exorcisms)
Sermon (*See* homily)
Service of the word (*synáxis*), 20
Sources of baptism
  New Testament, 14
  Old Testament, 13
Sunday Mass, 78
Symbolism in baptism
  "burial" in water, 32
  identification of humanity with Christ, 34
  image of Christ's death, 32
  participation of Christian in resurrection, 33

Symbolism in confirmation
  anointing, 56 f
  blow on cheek, 60
  imposition of hands, 56
  seal, 56, 60
Symbolism in Mass
  of eucharist, 96, 102
  offertory, the, 87 f
Synagogue service, 79 f

T

Tertullian, 2, 21, 30, 55, 56
Thanksgiving (*eucharistía*), 83
Thanksgiving after communion, 108
Theodore of Mopsuestia, 71
Thomas Aquinas, St., 41, 51, 57, 65, 66, 76, 105, 108
Torah, 14, 79
Transubstantiation, 106 f
Trent, Council of, 48, 58, 77, 95, 96, 103, 106
Trinity, 12, 15, 26, 37, 42, 73
Types of baptism
  bath of proselytes, 14
  ceremonial washings, 13
  crossing of Red Sea, 24, 29 f
  man born blind, 39

U

Unity of process of initiation, 2

V

Viaticum, 105
Vonier, Dom Anscar, 95

W

Water
  blessing of, 24 f
  living (i.e., running), 11, 38
  symbolism of, 10
White garments at baptism, 28
Word made flesh, 3

Y

Yahweh, 38, 52, 53, 54, 91

HEBREW, GREEK, AND LATIN WORDS AND PHRASES